Hearing God, Following the Spirit

"In our hyper-driven world, we regularly experience sensory overload and can feel spiritually overwhelmed. This calls us to a resilient faith where hearing from God rises above the noise. In this compelling book, readers can find a biblical, culturally attuned, and practical approach to hearing God's voice to make a difference in our world."

—**Ed Stetzer**, Talbot School of Theology

"Every generation needs its teachers who speak their language to interpret the times and help them learn to hear the voice of their Creator above the noise around them. In this era of constant distraction and disruption, Steven Félix-Jäger cuts through the chaos with a sound that is clear and that guides the reader to recognize the trustworthy Voice that matters most."

—**Tammy Dunahoo**, Portland Seminary, George Fox University

"At this critical turning point in history, few books cut through the noise with prophetic clarity. In *Hearing God, Following the Spirit*, Félix-Jäger brings hope, not by calling back to the past, but by placing waymarkers to help find the future. It is a thoughtful and accessible work created to help a generation not get lost in the wilderness. I definitely recommend."

—**Jessie Cruickshank**, pastor, founder of Whoology, and author of *Ordinary Discipleship: How God Wires Us for the Adventure of Transformation*

"Steven Félix-Jäger offers a thoughtful, timely, and engaging book on the crucial subject of Christian discernment in a pluralistic and post-truth age. With a rare combination of profound theological reflection, cultural analysis, and pastoral concern, Félix-Jäger provides a deeply insightful, compelling, and constructive exploration of how Christians might faithfully discern God's leading amid the pressures, confusions, and disinformation of contemporary life. This is a significant and rich contribution to an important conversation, and even readers who approach some of these issues from different theological traditions will find this volume stimulating, instructive, and well worth careful engagement."

—**John C. Peckham**, Andrews University

"The God who spoke in ancient times still has something to say in our day. But discerning God's voice among the many competing for our attention can be overwhelming. In his thought-provoking book, Félix-Jäger paves a way forward and shows us the importance of discerning the Spirit in a way that is consistent with the living Word of God, Jesus. Beautifully written and full of rich insight and philosophical depth, this book delivers complex concepts in easy-to-digest forms and provides creative and theologically grounded strategies to help us fully engage with what the Spirit is saying today."

—**Tania M. Harris**, practical theologian, author, and director of God Conversations, Sydney, Australia

"*Hearing God, Following the Spirit* achieves the Holy Grail of scholarship—offering rich theological insights with a warm, pastoral heart for the sake of practical, day-to-day discipleship. Félix-Jäger may be one of the premier Pentecostal theologians today, gifted with the ability to strike this uniquely difficult balance. You're in for a treat!"

—**Russell Joyce**, director of multiplication and expansion, the Foursquare Church; teaching pastor, B4 Church

Hearing God, Following the Spirit

Practicing Discernment in a Pluralistic Age

Steven Félix-Jäger

Baker Academic
a division of Baker Publishing Group
Grand Rapids, Michigan

© 2026 by Steven Félix-Jäger

Published by Baker Academic
a division of Baker Publishing Group
Grand Rapids, Michigan
BakerAcademic.com

Printed in the United States of America

All rights reserved. No part of this publication may be reproduced, stored in a retrieval system, or transmitted in any form or by any means—for example, electronic, photocopy, recording—without the prior written permission of the publisher. The only exception is brief quotations in printed reviews.

Library of Congress Cataloging-in-Publication Data
Names: Félix-Jäger, Steven author
Title: Hearing God, following the Spirit : practicing discernment in a pluralistic age / Steven Félix-Jäger.
Description: Grand Rapids, Michigan : Baker Academic, a division of Baker Publishing Group, [2026] | Includes bibliographical references and index.
Identifiers: LCCN 2026003945 | ISBN 9781540970329 paperback | ISBN 9781493455973 ebook | ISBN 9781493455980 pdf
Subjects: LCSH: Christianity and culture | Spiritual formation | Discernment (Christian theology)
Classification: LCC BR115.C8 F45 2026
LC record available at https://lccn.loc.gov/2026003945

Unless otherwise indicated, Scripture quotations are from the New Revised Standard Version Updated Edition. Copyright © 2021 National Council of Churches of Christ in the United States of America. Used by permission. All rights reserved worldwide.

Cover design by Studio Gearbox

Baker Publishing Group publications use paper produced from sustainable forestry practices and postconsumer waste whenever possible.

26 27 28 29 30 31 32 7 6 5 4 3 2 1

Contents

Acknowledgments ix

Introduction: Getting Lost in an Age of Pluralism 1

Part 1: Hearing God

1. Making Sense of Secularism 27
2. Hearing God in the Crowded Space of Competing Narratives 53
3. Hearing God Through the Noise of Misinformation 85

Part 2: Following the Spirit

4. Following the Spirit Past Political Tribalism 119
5. Following the Spirit When It's Dark 151

Conclusion: Being Led Through an Age of Discernment 181

Index 185

Acknowledgments

Hearing God through discernment is, in my view, one of the most important disciplines we can cultivate in our spiritual lives. Since each one of us must learn to walk in the Spirit and heed Christ's voice, I find it fitting to spend some time in these acknowledgments thanking the many people who have helped me hear God's voice more clearly.

I'd like to thank my father and my late mother, my sisters, aunts and uncles, nieces and nephews, and brothers-in-law. I'd like to thank dear friends from my days in Florida and now in California who have sought God with me. I'd like to thank the many colleagues and students who have joined me on this journey to know God deeper. And of course I'd like to thank my wife and daughter for not only seeking Jesus with me but loving and supporting me as I work out my calling as a scholar.

I'd also like to thank my friends who read all or parts of this book and gave me awesome feedback, especially Kevin Perales, Jen Thigpenn, Josh Edwards, Tim Lee, and Chandler Sargent, and the wonderful people at Baker Academic whom I've had the privilege of working with again, especially Brandy Scritchfield, Anna English, Kara Day, and Melisa Blok. You all are awesome.

Finally, I'd like to thank God, the subject of all my work. May we hear you clearly.

Introduction

Getting Lost in an Age of Pluralism

One of my earliest and most terrifying memories is when I got lost at the age of four. I grew up in Schillingsfürst, Germany, a tiny municipality in northwestern Bavaria. On weekends, my family often visited the nearby Rothenburg ob der Tauber, a stunning old town known for its beautifully preserved medieval architecture and storybook-like cobblestone lanes. Many of these lanes were blocked off from outside traffic, which made it easy for us to wander around and explore the shops and attractions.

One day, my family and I were strolling down one of these busy roads. Clutching my dad's hand, we wove through the bustling crowd of tourists and locals. Everything was moving so fast, and the town felt enormous! The half-timbered houses leaned over us, painted in pastel colors with rich brown trim. But somewhere between the chatter of the crowd and the scent of fresh pretzels and bratwursts, my little fingers slipped from my dad's grasp. It was okay, though. He was still right beside me—I could see his feet walking just a few inches from mine. Then he began to pick up speed. This felt weird. Why, all of a sudden, was he in such a hurry? I looked up, and my heart jumped out of my chest—those feet weren't my dad's! It all happened so fast. One moment, his reassuring hand was there; the next moment, I was racing through a crowd following some random guy I had thought was my dad. Soon I was swallowed by a tide of legs, coats, and towering strangers. I was lost.

It felt like hours, though it was probably only seconds, before I heard my dad's voice. He wasn't yelling, but he called my name in a tone so sharp with concern that it cut through the noise of the crowd. I turned, my heart racing, and there he was—my dad, pushing through the crowd to get me. "There you are," he said as he knelt down to pull me close. "You have to hold my hand tight or you might get lost!" It wasn't long before we were smiling again, and my fears faded into memory.

Sometimes I see this story repeating itself in my life today. In fact, this childhood story could be read as a parable for what it's like to hear and follow Jesus in today's perplexing age of pluralism. It's so easy to get lost. Whenever I loosen my grasp from God's leading hand, I'm instantly enveloped by people with their own goals and agendas scurrying from place to place. Multitudes of conversations fill the air around me so thickly that sometimes it becomes hard to discern Christ's clear and authoritative voice. Yet I know that Jesus's voice remains constant, and his hand is always reaching out. Sometimes, even as an adult, I just need to be pulled close and told to hold tight.

If any part of my story strikes a chord with you, know that you're not alone. Because today's age of pluralism can be overwhelming, learning to discern God's voice is our crucial task. This book isn't meant to be a step-by-step manual for navigating these extraordinary times. Instead, it emphasizes that the best guide isn't a list of strategies we might hear in a sermon, podcast, or a book like this but the Holy Spirit of God who is actively revealing Christ to us and in us today. Since God is triune, it's perfectly appropriate to refer to the Holy Spirit as the Spirit of Christ. The Holy Spirit brings Christ into our daily lives (John 14:16–18) and allows us to experience his fullness (Gal. 2:20; Col. 1:27). And it's through the Spirit of Christ that we come to know the Father. That's why Paul reminds us, "because you are children, God has sent the Spirit of his Son into our hearts, crying, 'Abba! Father!'" (Gal. 4:6).[1] This book should therefore not be viewed as a replacement for God's guidance or as a means to undermine discernment. Instead, it stands as a testament to our true guide—the Spirit of Christ—and considers how the Spirit has equipped us with discernment to recognize Jesus's voice today.

This book deals theologically *with* culture, but since it doesn't have a particular theological method, we shouldn't really call it a theology *of* culture. Rather, it should be seen as a pastoral and theological response to culture, one that blends insights from cultural analysis and philosophy with traditional Christian fields like theology and spiritual formation. It's written for anyone interested in exploring what the Spirit is doing in the world today. The rest of this introductory chapter will profile today's era, explore what pluralism is, and ponder what it means to live in such a time as this. The next section will look at how the Spirit ought to be *every* Christian's guide and why discernment is the crucial spiritual discipline and gift for an age of pluralism. Finally, the last section will wrap up with a brief outline of the structure and main points of the book.

New Challenges in a New Era

Does this era seem particularly difficult for you to hear God? It often does for me. In this fast-paced, tech-oriented reality, life can feel insanely complicated when we are bombarded with endless information, choices, and opinions. When we think about earlier decades of our lives, it might seem like the world drew clearer lines between right and wrong. Everything felt more stable because roles and expectations were more clearly and rigidly defined. We understood what was expected of us and what our place was in the world. But as we reminisce, are we just reflecting some cognitive bias? Are we looking back with nostalgia because we fear what's ahead of us? The present might feel overwhelming because we're right in the thick of it, and

1. All Scripture references are from the NRSVue unless otherwise noted.

the past might look simple in hindsight. But from a distance many details get blurred and forgotten. We can't let nostalgia blind us to the fact that every time period comes with its own set of challenges.

Yet there certainly are real challenges to hearing God and following the Spirit today. We're facing things we've never faced before. I'd like to suggest that today's unique challenges stem from our living in a radically pluralized era—one of the first claims of this book. I'll break down what that means later on, but for now, just know that **pluralism** refers to a social condition where different groups, cultures, identities, and practices exist side by side. We've stepped into an age of pluralism because we have both global cultural diversity and varied technological means to connect with these cultures and share information. As such, we're in a time when many voices are vying for our attention all at once. The goal of this book is to help us figure out how to recognize, hear, and respond[2] to God's voice amid the noise.

Interpreting Culture

Karl Barth, arguably one of the greatest Protestant theologians, famously advised young theologians by saying, "Take your Bible and take your newspaper, and read both. But interpret newspapers from your Bible."[3] This quote highlights how crucial it is for our theology to connect with the world we inhabit. Theology shouldn't just focus on abstract ideas about God but should actively confront real-world challenges by engaging politics, culture, and social issues. Coming from Barth, this isn't mere advice for theologians to stay relevant—it calls for a deep responsibility to meet, interpret, and expound on the day's most pressing issues. Barth lived through some extremely chaotic

2. The three disciplines of recognizing, hearing, and responding to God's voice as a way to understand divine revelatory experience are drawn from Tania Harris, *Hearing God's Voice: Towards a Theology of Contemporary Pentecostal Revelatory Experience* (Brill, 2023), 119.

3. The phrase is commonly linked to Barth; however, the precise wording and context remains dubious. In a 1963 *Time Magazine* article, Barth recalls having offered this advice to young theologians forty years prior. You can read the story here: "Barth in Retirement," *Time*, May 31, 1963, https://time.com/archive/6831843/barth-in-retirement.

times that included World War I, the rise of the Nazi Party in Germany, World War II, and the Cold War. In 1934, he played a key role in creating the Barmen Declaration, a theological declaration written by a group of Protestant church leaders who repudiated Nazi influence on German Christianity. Some of his theological writings also tackled the urgent issues of his era, especially the moral and political dilemmas brought on by totalitarian governments and modern secularism.[4] Barth's public engagement was clear, courageous, and prophetic.

The problem with Barth's famous quote is not what he meant by it but its relevance for today. Since we've democratized our news outlets, we don't get much of our news from newspapers anymore. Instead, we have highly partisan news television, YouTube channels, Reddit, TikTok, and podcasts.[5] The explosion of digital media, citizen journalism, and social networks has completely changed how we get and share information. However, this flood of information has also opened the door to misinformation, disinformation, echo chambers, and ever-increasing divisions. Many churchgoers and even some pastors find it tough to grasp what's happening in the world today. It's not that we don't know how to read and interpret the Bible (though that can happen too); it's that we struggle to properly read and interpret culture, making us prone to leaning on stereotypes or making ill-informed assumptions. We end up trying to share biblical truths while inadvertently strengthening biases and reinforcing social walls. But before we jump into the difficulties of interpreting culture, let's take a moment to define what our particular era looks like.

Defining Our Era

When I say we're in an age of pluralism, I don't mean we're in an era of religious pluralism (although this is also evident in many

4. This is particularly evident in Barth's *The Epistle to the Romans*. See Karl Barth, *The Epistle to the Romans* (Oxford University Press, 1968), 74.

5. See Craig T. Robertson, "People Are Turning Away from the News. Here's Why It May Be Happening," Reuters Institute, February 21, 2025, https://reutersinstitute.politics.ox.ac.uk/news/people-are-turning-away-news-heres-why-it-may-be-happening.

parts of the world). Religious pluralism acknowledges that various faiths and beliefs can coexist peacefully in a society or community, as demonstrated in the many different religious symbols that make up the "coexist" bumper stickers. However, religious pluralism goes beyond mere tolerance; it's about getting involved and having interreligious dialogues between various faiths. Some thinkers, like theologian John Hick, even argue that all religions at their core point toward the same ultimate reality.[6] That is not my argument. In fact, later in this book (chap. 2) I argue that we must avoid sentiments like Hick's, recognizing the exclusivity of Christ as we follow the Spirit's global, ecumenical work that seeks to draw all people to Jesus.

As hinted above, I'm using the sociological sense of the term "pluralism," which highlights the fact that we live in a world that's hyperconnected—one that recognizes all sorts of customs, traditions, languages, ethics, religions, economies, and governments. This idea of pluralism doesn't suggest that all cultures mix into one big stew to form a super-culture. Instead, it sees cultures existing side by side, engaging with and impacting each other, whether by embracing differences or resisting external influences. Our particular views of the world are heavily impacted by the intertwined, sometimes conflicting relationships between different social systems. Thus, today's state of pluralism can be seen as a web of different worlds. There's no single all-encompassing system that rules over everything else. Instead, various smaller systems exist together within a broader global framework. The social interactions happening in a complex global scene define the new collective experience we're in—an **age of pluralism**.

A major reason we're pluralist is because we're globalized. **Globalization** is happening on both economic and cultural levels, essentially spreading modern systems across the globe.[7] These modern systems include free-market capitalism, global supply chains, e-commerce platforms, international trade regulations, global governmental

6. John Hick, "Whatever Path Men Choose Is Mine," *Modern Churchman* 18, nos. 1–2 (1974): 11.

7. Michael Wilkinson, "What's Global About Global Pentecostalism?," *Journal of Pentecostal Theology* 17 (2008): 97.

frameworks like the United Nations, and so on. Culturally, globalization unites us through shared values found in religion, pop culture, and tourism, creating social bonds between us that might not exist otherwise. How many of us learned about Hinduism from movies like *Life of Pi* (2012) or about contemporary East Asian cultures from *Crazy Rich Asians* (2018)? Kids today are surrounded by global influences every day too. Just ask my ten-year-old daughter after she finishes watching *Bluey*, playing Pokémon, or jamming out to Stray Kids. Globalization is not a trend that will fade away but a significant force shaping our current era.

One of the biggest drivers of rapid globalization in recent years is technology. With advancements in information tech and telecommunications, countries and cultures can connect more frequently and effectively.[8] Easy access to online information and instant communication through tech-based platforms have expanded our perceptions of time and space. We can keep tabs on events happening anywhere in the world at any moment, so that even as the global population grows, our understanding of the world feels smaller. And with the ability to interact with various cultures across the globe, people are gaining a deeper understanding of the beliefs that define different groups. Instead of depending on exaggerated portrayals in traditional media or secondhand stories from someone's travels, we can simply grab our phones, pull up a livestream, and witness firsthand what's actually shaping other cultures. Today's world is pluralistic not because everyone is diluting their religious and cultural identities but because they are understanding the diverse, genuine lifestyles that exist worldwide. As the West becomes more open to global perspectives, it's realizing that it's part of a vast community filled with various worldviews. In this pluralistic landscape, we face the challenge of figuring out how to exist and thrive alongside a multitude of competing narratives.

8. Stella Aririguzoh, "Communication Competencies, Culture and SDGs: Effective Processes to Cross-Cultural Communication," *Humanities & Social Sciences Communications* 9, no. 96 (2022): 2.

On a positive note, globalization and technology have significantly ramped up our social awareness in the West. With a broader perspective, we can spot both the positive and the negative impacts our policies make globally. Being more informed helps us recognize social and environmental issues as they happen, which motivates us to take action. Recently, there's been a noticeable increase in humanitarian efforts, and research indicates that we're becoming more mindful consumers.[9] Social activists like Greta Thunberg (Swedish climate activist), Malala Yousafzai (Pakistani education activist), and Ai Weiwei (Chinese artist and human rights activist) are making global headlines. This growing social awareness comes as a result of engaging with the world, helping us move away from the idea of linear progress and Western superiority and reimagine the West as part of a global community.

You might think that the push for global influence and international ties has made national identities less prevalent. However, there's a growing backlash against globalization that reinforces nationalistic sentiments. Today, we're seeing the rise of fundamentalisms, which make the world seem simple and easy to grasp through a "strict and literal adherence to a set of basic principles."[10] Nationalism, in this sense, is a political fundamentalism, similar to religious fundamentalism, which rejects the complex exchange of values and ideas across cultures.[11] As people learn that the world is much bigger and more complicated than they ever imagined, they may cling to nationalism to both simplify the world and to protect their identity from the impact of other cultures. A lot of Western nations, like the US, are embracing postliberal social ideas that promote greater focus on nationalistic unity and the needs of its own people. Therefore, in an ironic twist, this pluralist era has also opened the door for sentiments that push back against globalization.

9. Colin Wong, "2025 Consumer Insights Predictions," Greenbook, January 8, 2025, https://www.greenbook.org/insights/focus-on-apac/2025-consumer-insights-prediction.

10. *Merriam-Webster Dictionary*, "fundamentalism," accessed December 17, 2025, https://www.merriam-webster.com/dictionary/fundamentalism.

11. Thorsten Botz-Bornstein, *The New Aesthetics of Deculturation: Neoliberalism, Fundamentalism and Kitsch* (Bloomsbury Academic, 2019), 5.

As we can see, there are numerous challenges ahead of us, including global exposure, religious diversity, misinformation, and a bunch of -isms (relativism, nationalism, secularism, reductionism, etc.). Yet we should find comfort in the fact that the Spirit was present and at work in every era, just as the Spirit is present and at work among us today. Think of it like walking up to a sprawling maze. Before jumping into the maze, you might find yourself feeling overwhelmed by the twists and turns that lie ahead. What if you lose your way? What if the paths lead you in circles? But then it hits you: This maze is meant to challenge you, not trap you! There's always a way out, no matter how lost or confused you might feel. Each wrong turn is just another part of the maze unfolding, bringing you closer to uncovering its secrets. All you need is some courage, determination, and maybe a little help when the walls seem to close in. In our maze of global pluralism, that help comes from the Spirit; we just need to be aware and obedient to follow where the Spirit is leading.

A Theological Response

The best way to navigate an age of pluralism is not to try to control the situation by our own means but to tap into what the Spirit is doing in the world. Imagine you're in a small boat in rough waters. The water feels like it's got a mind of its own, daring you to either press on or head back. If we had the power, we'd calm those storms like Jesus did or magically create safe shores. But if we were on the boat with a skilled captain, the smart move would be to relax and let the captain steer the boat through the chaos. As we navigate an age of pluralism, we need to let God guide our ships. We need to let God's vision for our lives become our own. Of course, this means we need to be able to hear God first—we can't act in obedience if we never hear God's call. This is why discernment is the answer for our era. Without it, even if we do hear God, we might miss recognizing God's voice through the noise.

Discernment is being able to comprehend things that are unclear. This book takes a fresh look at discernment and the spiritual practices associated with it for our pluralistic age. While there are some fantastic reads out there about discerning God's voice, most of them lean heavily into spiritual formation. For instance, Dallas Willard's *Hearing God* and Henri Nouwen's *Discernment* explore the ways in which people can attune themselves to God in their own spiritual journeys. These classic works are significant contributions to the discipline of spiritual formation but focus mainly on nurturing one's inner spiritual life. In contrast, this book aims to weave together cultural studies—tackling the complexities of our pluralistic era—with spiritual formation and theology. Willard's and Nouwen's books are designed to be generally applicable in any era, but this book zeros in on the nuances of our current era. It does two main things: It analyzes our cultural landscape and provides a theological and pastoral response to its challenges. It informs us about the world in which God calls us to be witnesses.

In talking about spiritual discernment and being led by the Spirit, we must begin with **pneumatology**—the theological study of the Holy Spirit. Historically, the Spirit has been the most overlooked person of the Trinity. Early theologians usually tackled theology in a systematic way, starting with the Father and moving on to the Son. Sadly, by the time they got to the Spirit, their discussions were often lacking.[12] It's only in the last fifty years, especially with the growth of Pentecostal studies,[13] that the Spirit has started to get an appropriate

12. For instance, Origen, a third-century theologian, made notable advancements in trinitarian theology; however, his work on the Spirit was briefer than his work on the Father and the *Logos* (the Son). One of the most important works on the Trinity, Augustine's *On the Trinity* (fifth century), discussed the Spirit primarily in relational terms as the bond of love uniting the Father and the Son, rather than providing a comprehensive account of the Spirit's personhood and functions. Finally, the original version of the Nicene Creed (325 CE) had just a single line about the Holy Spirit: "And in the Holy Spirit." Yet there were elaborate descriptions of the Father and the Son, which covered things like Christ's divinity, his part in creation, his incarnation, and his resurrection.

13. For example, see Walter Hollenweger, *Pentecostalism: Origins and Developments Worldwide* (Hendrickson, 1997); William Menzies and Robert Menzies, *Spirit and Power: Foundations of Pentecostal Experience* (Zondervan, 2000); and Amos Yong, *The Spirit Poured Out on All Flesh: Pentecostalism and the Possibility of Global Theology* (Baker Academic, 2005).

amount of attention. Many theologians from various fields are now seeking to understand the person and work of the Spirit.[14]

Trinitarian theology focuses on both the unity of and the distinctions within the Godhead. God isn't a mix of parts but is one in essence. The titles Father, Son, and Spirit, along with phrases like "only begotten" (John 3:16 KJV) and "proceeds" (15:26 CSB) or "goes out from" (NIV), highlight their relationships, showing distinctions without implying separation. The Father, Son, and Spirit are co-eternal and co-equal in dignity and status; all worthy of worship. They work together in harmony, sharing essence, power, and will. Still, their roles are unique; for instance, it was the Son who became a man in Jesus Christ, not the Father or the Spirit. However, both the Father and the Spirit played a part in the Son's incarnation, as seen during events like Jesus's baptism and transfiguration. When it comes to God's relation to humanity, the Spirit is the one who makes the triune God personal for believers. Theologian Millard Erickson points out that while the Father is perceived as transcendent and the Son seems historically distant, the Spirit lives within believers, making God's presence real and accessible.[15]

Across both Testaments, the Spirit is involved in triune actions that reflect God's mission. In the Old Testament, the Spirit acts as a creative force (Gen. 1:2; Job 26:13) and nurturer of life (Gen. 6:3; Job 27:3; 33:4; 34:14; Ps. 104:29–30; Eccles. 12:7; Isa. 42:5). The Spirit inspires individuals (Exod. 28:3; Num. 11:17; Judg. 3:10; 1 Sam. 10:5–11; 2 Sam. 23:2; 1 Chron. 12:18; 2 Chron. 20:14; 24:20; Neh. 9:19–31; Isa. 44:3) and empowers people (Mic. 3:8; Zech. 4:6). By the time we reach the New Testament, the Spirit's role is clearer and even more vital to the community of believers after the death and resurrection of Jesus. The Spirit not only supports and empowers (Acts 1–2) but

14. For example, see Jack Deere, *Surprised by the Power of the Holy Spirit: A Former Dallas Seminary Professor Discovers That God Still Speaks and Heals Today* (Zondervan, 1993); Jürgen Moltmann, *The Source of Life: The Holy Spirit and the Theology of Life* (Fortress, 1997); and Clark Pinnock, *Flame of Love: A Theology of the Holy Spirit* (InterVarsity, 1996).

15. Millard Erickson, *Introducing Christian Doctrine*, 3rd ed., ed. L. Arnold Hustad (Baker Academic, 2015), 296.

also transforms believers into living temples of God's presence (1 Cor. 3:16). This change signifies a momentous transition, as being indwelt by the Spirit marks God's people both in the New Testament and now.

Moving forward, we should reflect on how being indwelt by the Spirit *is* the solution to our concerns about our current age. Consider what Paul tells the Roman church:

> But you are not in the flesh; you are in the Spirit, since the Spirit of God dwells in you. Anyone who does not have the Spirit of Christ does not belong to him. But if Christ is in you, then the body is dead because of sin, but the Spirit is life because of righteousness. If the Spirit of him who raised Jesus from the dead dwells in you, he who raised Christ Jesus from the dead will give life to your mortal bodies also through his Spirit that dwells in you. (Rom. 8:9–11)

Let's stop and soak in what Paul says in verse 11: "The Spirit of him who raised Jesus from the dead dwells in you." That's huge! The core belief for all Christians is that the Holy Spirit of God, the very same Spirit that brought Jesus back to life, lives within us. If that's the case, then God can effectively execute any mission through us. Yet God has given us free will and thus desires our voluntary submission to our calling. In other words, the Spirit of God dwells in us, but we must submit to God's will in our lives to truly walk in lockstep with God. Hence, our tasks are to recognize and hear God's voice and then to be obedient to God's will, knowing that being able to discern God's voice at all is a work of the Spirit.

The Spirit Is for Everyone

I'm a card-carrying Pentecostal. I would say this is only a figure of speech, but I actually do have a card that I keep in my wallet. The front of it says "Esteban (Steven) Felix-Jager is under appointment and is hereby certified as a Licensed Minister in good standing." That's right, I'm a licensed minister in a classical Pentecostal denomination. I teach at a Pentecostal university, and I lead worship and periodically preach at a Pentecostal church. There are important practical and theological reasons I'm a Pentecostal: I love our expressive, embodied worship, our Spirit-centric focus on mission, our egalitarian values, our high regard for the Bible, and our boldness to seek healings and miracles through prayer. Yet I'm also critical of various aspects of Pentecostalism. I'm not a fan of the hard prosperity-gospel teachings[16] or triumphalist postures that sometimes creep into our tradition. I'm cautious about any of our ties to dominion theology. I'm disappointed by the anti-intellectual attitudes that pop up in our churches, and I can't stand how our tradition can get politicized.[17] I point this out not only to honestly express my own positionality but also to show that it's possible for us to be proud of our own tradition while critiquing the things we believe undermine its strengths. This is the sort of critical eye we'll need as we look at how various unbiblical ideologies challenge and at times enter the logics of our faith traditions. If we take this honest approach, I believe we'll be able to see what the Spirit is doing in the world and even in our own backyards.

An Interdenominational Case for the Spirit

While I glean much from the things I learned from Pentecostalism, throughout this book I would like to make an interdenominational case for the Spirit and confidently say that *every Christian should be a Spirit-filled Christian*. Does this mean I believe every Christian should

16. Kate Bowler argues that although prosperity teachings focus on faith, wealth, health, and success, it's useful to differentiate between "hard" and "soft" prosperity. Supporters of hard prosperity view faith as a strict law, meaning that any setbacks indicate the believer didn't have the requisite faith. In contrast, soft prosperity embraces the idea of an abundant life but doesn't treat prosperity principles as strict and unyielding, like those who follow hard prosperity do. See Kate Bowler, *Blessed: A History of the American Prosperity Gospel* (Oxford University Press, 2013), 97.

17. Dominion theology claims that Christians have the authority to influence and transform society based on biblical teachings. It looks at Gen. 1:28, where people are told to "have dominion" over the earth, as a directive for believers to make an impact in all sectors of society including the government, culture, and education. Matthew D. Taylor's *The Violent Take It by Force* traces the influence of dominion theology to all sectors of evangelicalism, in which he includes Charismatic Christianity and Pentecostalism. See Matthew D. Taylor, *The Violent Take It by Force: The Christian Movement That Is Threatening Our Democracy* (Broadleaf Books, 2024), 67–70.

be denominationally Pentecostal? No. Paul's famous body metaphor (Rom. 12:3–9; 1 Cor. 6:9–20; Eph. 4:11–16; Col. 1:15–20) offers us some valuable insights here. He compares the church to a body made up of various members, each with its own role. While every member serves a different purpose, they're all essential parts of the same body. One way to look at these passages is to see our various Christian denominations or theological traditions as unique yet equally vital to the global church. Each tradition contributes something special, and together they form a strong, unified body. The church is Christ's, so despite its variety, Christ remains the head of the universal church.

As is often done in **ecclesiology** (the theological study of the church), we can differentiate between the visible and invisible church to better grasp the nature of each one. The **visible church** is the organized, outward manifestation of the church that includes everyone who claims to be a Christian and participates in church services and activities, and it is often linked to a particular church or denomination. By contrast, the **invisible church** is the church's spiritual reality that is only known by God. It consists of all genuine believers throughout time who are united to Christ through faith, no matter their church or denomination. While the visible church is today's platform for sharing the gospel and welcoming people into the invisible church, the invisible church embodies the real unity of believers. This book is intended for everyone who is listening for God today in the universal, visible church, since we are all united in Christ's invisible church. That being said, an important point to consider in this discussion is the church's origin at Pentecost.

If you attend a Pentecostal church service, you'll hear mentions of Pentecost in no time. The same goes for any Pentecostal theology book; you won't get far into the introduction without a deep exegetical dive into Acts 2. However, it's important to remember that Pentecost isn't just for Pentecostals—it's a narrative that belongs to the whole church. Acts 2 tells us that the Spirit was poured out on all flesh and that everyone who was present in the upper room began to speak in tongues (v. 4). These were "xenolalic" tongues, meaning they were actual languages that the speakers hadn't learned before. The tongues made it possible for the believers to share the gospel with a crowd from various nations that spoke different languages. Through this, the Spirit not only brought people together by allowing them to proclaim the good news in a multiplicity of ways but also gave them the strength to carry out the Great Commission. With three thousand people coming to faith that day, Pentecost is seen by most Christians as the birth of the universal church (v. 41).

But Pentecostals have a special take on Acts 2. They view it as the beginning of their own journey that's still unfolding today. Pentecostals believe that the Spirit poured out at Pentecost isn't just a one-off event with a definitive ending. Rather, they see the outpour as continual: The church today is being poured into by the same Spirit that Christ poured out on all flesh. Why do Pentecostals see it this way? Well, in Acts 2:17–18, Peter references Joel 2:28–29 and points out that Pentecost points to a fulfillment for "the last days." For Pentecostals, the last days cover the whole time from Pentecost to Christ's return, suggesting that the outpouring is ongoing. In verse 38, Peter says, "Repent and be baptized every one of you in the name of Jesus Christ so that your sins may be forgiven, and you will receive the gift of the Holy Spirit." He then explicitly states that this promised gift is for them, their children, and everyone far away—meaning, presumably, anyone throughout time who answers God's call. Although this is how Pentecostals often read Acts 2, one implication is that the Spirit is poured out on *all* flesh and thus is continually poured out on the whole church. That means the Spirit was and is poured out on Presbyterians, Methodists, Baptists, Catholics, and Orthodox. We can thus make the interdenominational claim that every Christian should be a Spirit-filled Christian.

The church is a key character in God's narrative that steps into the spotlight at Pentecost. Ever since that moment, the church has been woven into every part of the redemption story and will keep playing a role as it anticipates Christ's return. For Pentecostals, the church's journey is still unfolding, even though the people who make up the visible church change with each generation. It's kind of like the classic Bond movies. The early ones, starting with *Dr. No* (1962), had a recurring cast of characters (think M, Q, and Miss Moneypenny). Across the film series, James Bond remains the same character no matter who takes on the role, whether it's Sean Connery or Roger Moore. If the early church was like Sean Connery, maybe we're in the Pierce Brosnan phase now[18]—but it's still the same Bond who's shooting at the camera in those iconic opening scenes.

Since all Christians are part of the Acts 2 experience, it's worth diving into what this passage says about hearing God. Verses 1–4 explain how the Spirit empowers believers to hear God's voice in unexpected, sometimes supernatural ways. In verses 6–8, we see that God communicates in ways that are accessible to all. At Pentecost, people from various languages and backgrounds hear God's wonders in their own tongues, proving that God meets people where they are and speaks in ways they can grasp. In verses 17–18, Peter quotes Joel in saying, "Your sons and your daughters shall prophesy, and your young men shall see visions, and your old men shall dream dreams. Even upon my slaves, both men and women, in those days I will pour out my Spirit, and they shall prophesy." Hearing God can come through prophetic insights, visions, and dreams inspired by the Spirit, and verses 37–38 reveal that when the crowd hears this, they are deeply moved and ask Peter and the apostles, "Brothers, what should we do?" Peter replies, "Repent and be baptized every one of you in the name of Jesus Christ so that your sins may be forgiven, and you will receive the gift of the Holy Spirit." These verses show that truly hearing God goes beyond just understanding; it demands a genuine response. The crowd's question reflects their awareness of God's voice and their readiness to obey. And in verses 41–47, through the many conversions at Pentecost, we see how hearing God's voice leads to life-changing transformation. So, hearing God brings people together into God's family.

18. Astute Bond fans might have noticed that I left out Daniel Craig's Bond. That's because Craig's Bond started a brand-new Bond timeline, whereas the Bonds from Connery to Brosnan were all part of the same continuous story. I really like Craig as Bond, but unfortunately his story betrays the point I'm trying to make!

The book of John is also important for understanding the Spirit's role in hearing God. In it, we see the Spirit portrayed as God's advocate and counselor. Throughout chapters 14–16, Jesus refers to the Spirit as the "paraclete" (*paraklētos*). This Greek term has been translated as "helper," "comforter," "counselor," "friend," and "advocate," and all these translations point to the idea that the Spirit, as paraclete, is God right there with us, helping and guiding us. In John 14:15–17, Jesus mentions that he will send the Spirit of truth. In a true demonstration of the Trinity, Jesus is saying *he's* the current paraclete for the disciples, and when he's gone, the Father will send them another paraclete who will stay with them forever: the Spirit. Jesus embodies the truth, and the Spirit continues Christ's work with the disciples by leading them into all truth (14:15–18; 15:26; 16:12–14). The Spirit helps them remember Jesus's teachings (14:26), testifies about him (15:26), reveals truth from both the Son and the Father (14:26; 15:26; 16:13), and is sent by the Father in Jesus's name (14:26). Pentecostals would say that the promise of the paraclete was not just for the disciples but for all believers, as we are all indwelt by the Spirit.

The Spirit also gives us spiritual gifts to strengthen the church, help others, honor God, and carry out God's mission here on earth (1 Cor. 12; Eph. 4; 1 Pet. 4). The gifts include faith, knowledge, healing, and wisdom. Each gift serves a unique role, but they all work together to edify the church internally and promote it through witness and evangelism. As we've mentioned before, out of all these gifts, the gift of discernment might be the most important for tuning into what God is saying in our current pluralistic age.

Discernment as Spiritual Discipline and Spiritual Gift

An interdenominational approach for hearing God's voice begins with the recognition of discernment as both a spiritual *discipline* and a spiritual *gift*. We often only think of discernment as a spiritual discipline that everyone can adopt. While that's true, it's important to remember that discernment is among the spiritual gifts Paul mentions in 1 Corinthians 12:10 and 28, where he also lists various gifts like administration, healing, interpretation, tongues, prophecy, wisdom, apostleship, faith, helps, knowledge, miracles, and teaching. Many of these gifts are meant to be lived out in our daily Christian lives. For instance, as we strive to become more like Christ, we should grow in wisdom, faith, and knowledge. The same goes for discernment; we should aim to hear God's voice more clearly each day. So what really sets these apart as spiritual gifts?

I see the difference between a general spiritual discipline and a spiritual gift as a special impartation. Discernment as a spiritual discipline involves growing in wisdom, making thoughtful decisions through prayer, and diving into Scripture to distinguish right from wrong or good from better. It's something every believer should pursue to deepen their faith (Heb. 5:14). The *gift* of discernment, however, is a special ability given by the Spirit that doesn't depend on logic or personal experiences. It is a direct result of the Spirit's work, transcending human reasoning, gut feelings, or anything we've learned (1 Cor. 12:10).

The spiritual gift of discernment allows us to sense the presence and influence of spiritual forces—whether divine or demonic—in various situations, people, or places. For instance, someone with this gift might be able to tell if a teaching or prophecy is genuinely from God, just a human idea, or influenced by something evil. To put it succinctly, the **spiritual gift of discernment** is a supernatural ability granted to some for the church's benefit, especially during times of spiritual need. Meanwhile, the **spiritual discipline of discernment** is a skill that all believers should cultivate through prayer, Scripture study, and wise decision-making for spiritual growth.

Considering these distinctions, I would like to make two points. First, *both* are of the Spirit and fall under the category of pneumatology. The discipline of discernment concerns learning to hear God in our everyday lives. It's about syncing our spirits with God's Spirit on a daily basis. And the gift of discernment is given to us by the Spirit as we are given the ability to recognize the spiritual forces at play in the world. Second, both the spiritual discipline and the spiritual gift of discernment are crucial in our age of pluralism. Not only do we need to be able to recognize the invisible forces at work in the world today, but we must also grow in our sensitivity to hearing God in our personal spiritual formation. Throughout this book, we will spend more time discussing ways to cultivate the discipline of discernment, but we will not forget how important it is to seek and pray for the gift of discernment—both are crucial for our current day.

Henri Nouwen describes discernment beautifully when he says it "allows us to 'see through' the appearance of things to their deeper meaning and come to know the interworkings of God's love and our own unique place in the world. . . . Perceiving, seeing through, understanding, and being aware of God's presence are what is meant by discernment."[19] Nouwen is primarily talking about the spiritual discipline of discernment and goes on to advise important contemplative practices to hone it. But I think Nouwen's quote works equally well for the spiritual gift of discernment, which also allows us to see through the appearance of things. Through the gift of discernment, we can recognize when God is moving in and through a person or situation, whether they are driven by fleshly desires, or if they're showcasing a counterfeit work of the devil. Because our pluralistic age is full of flesh and spirits, the key to hearing God's voice and following the Spirit is discernment.

Structure of the Book

As I've mentioned throughout this introduction, this book aims to help readers listen to God speak through the multitude of surrounding voices and follow the Spirit while navigating the various twists and turns of the winding paths ahead. To achieve this goal, the remainder of this book is split into two parts that deal with hearing God and following the Spirit.

19. Henri Nouwen, *Discernment: Reading the Signs of Daily Life* (HarperOne, 2013), 6.

Part 1: Hearing God

The first chapter of part 1 is called "Making Sense of Secularism." This chapter questions if our society is truly as secular as many claim. While secularity has influenced all parts of Western society, it's more accurate to view our society as pluralistic rather than just secular. Living in a pluralistic age means we simultaneously encounter a vast array of religious, philosophical, and political voices, and we can tend to see everything, even the secular, as spiritual. As discerners, our role is to identify the types of spirituality we'll engage with and endorse. An important part of discerning God's voice is being able to tell when our revelatory experiences are actually God speaking. Recognizing God's voice and knowing God's personality requires deep and constant prayer in the Spirit—it requires knowing God on an intimate level.[20]

Chapter 2 is called "Hearing God in the Crowded Space of Competing Narratives." The constant barrage of conflicting accounts of what's true and how we should respond religiously to certain things can leave us feeling spiritually confused. To tackle this, we'll explore the concepts of particularism and religious pluralism, looking at what it means to affirm the particularity of Christ while also acknowledging the Spirit's efforts around the world. In a pluralistic world, the Spirit empowers us to do more than just speak to the religious other; it helps us listen and learn from others too, recognizing God's voice even in unexpected places. To hear God's voice clearly in any dialogue, we must internalize the Christian narrative found in Scripture. Therefore, a spiritual reading of Scripture is crucial for establishing a narrative base for our discernment. By recognizing the cultural lenses we read Scripture through, we can trust that the Spirit transcends whatever perspectives we're bound by.

Finally, part 1 wraps up with a chapter called "Hearing God Through the Noise of Misinformation," which argues that in our post-truth era, truth is cheapened and reduced by social media

20. Admittedly, this first chapter gets a little philosophically dense at times, but please push through! I promise it'll all make sense in the end.

echoing our own biases back to us. This casts us into a cycle of self-absorption, where we become our own authorities of truth and judges of morality. As mis- and disinformation arise, we begin to distrust authorities. While we should thoughtfully engage with genuine doubts and questions about our faith, the sheer mass of rootless and uncritical information we encounter every day can obscure what it means to follow Christ. Therefore, part 1 argues that authenticity is vital for sharing any socioreligious ideas that might impact others. It considers the types of authorities we might give ear to alongside the Spirit and Scripture, recognizing that the Spirit is our ultimate authority for all things.

Part 2: Following the Spirit

Part 2 kicks off with a chapter titled "Following the Spirit Past Political Tribalism," which discusses what it means to be Spirit-led through the chaos of coercive politics. The world tells us to use political buzzwords as identity markers to both label and discard people. Yet in a time when we're encouraged to see others as political foes, we're called to be ministers of reconciliation (2 Cor. 5:18). Following the Spirit means setting our sights on what's real and not illusory. It means choosing God's kingdom, which is good, pure, and everlasting, instead of any earthly kingdom that is shallow, power-hungry, and unjust. It means treating people as citizens of heaven, either lost or found, rather than as earthly enemies. When political tribes try to name and claim us, we must double down on the identity God has given us. We are beloved children of God, submitted to the lordship of Christ. The spiritual discipline of worship helps us reinforce our identity in Christ and is one of the most effective ways to avert the malformation of political tribalism.

Part 2 concludes with a chapter called "Following the Spirit When It's Dark," which zeros in on what it means to be Spirit-led when it feels like God is MIA or just doesn't seem to care about our struggles—times when we ask, *Why isn't God answering our prayers?* I'll argue that even when God seems silent, the Spirit continues to guide us—and worship can offer us a space to encounter God, remember who we are, and be renewed even when it's dark. This final chapter reframes worship as a form of "holy play," a sacred and imaginative space where healing and hope can emerge amid anxiety and dread. Appropriately, it is a conversation about faithfulness through crisis that rounds out this entire book. In the end, faithfully following the Spirit through any circumstance is, ultimately, an act of discernment in a pluralistic age.

The conclusion proposes that we reconceptualize our current age of pluralism as an age of discernment. This shift alters our perspective from a fear-inducing sociopolitical frame to a hope-building theological frame. As Christians, it's important that we perceive the world in alignment with God's vision, and we do this by discerning and joining the Spirit's work in the world.

Conclusion

If we think back to the story I told at the start of this introduction, trying to hear my dad's voice in the crowd is like hearing God today, and holding his hand to navigate the throngs of people is akin to following the Spirit. The sort of Spirit-filled discernment we need in our age of pluralism comes through the disciplines of prayer and spiritual reading and through responding to God's voice by worshiping in the Spirit. Taking Barth's advice, this introduction took the Bible in one hand to understand the Spirit and took the newspaper in the other to understand culture. The rest of this book will similarly look to interpret culture through the Word *and* the Spirit.

KEY WORDS

- **age of pluralism**: An era defined by the social interactions happening in a complex global scene
- **discernment**: Being able to comprehend things that are unclear
- **ecclesiology**: The theological study of the church
- **globalization**: The process of spreading modern systems across the globe
- **invisible church**: The church's spiritual reality that is only truly known by God
- **pluralism**: A social condition where different groups, cultures, identities, and practices exist side by side
- **pneumatology**: The theological study of the Holy Spirit
- **spiritual discipline of discernment**: A skill for clarity that all believers should cultivate, involving prayer, Scripture study, and wise decision-making for spiritual growth
- **spiritual gift of discernment**: A supernatural ability for clarity granted to some for the church's benefit, especially during times of spiritual need
- **visible church**: The organized, outward manifestation of the church

DISCUSSION QUESTIONS

- Do any characteristics of our age of pluralism make you uneasy? Which ones?
- In what ways does modern technology amplify both the benefits and the challenges of living in an age of pluralism?
- This introduction contrasts discernment as a spiritual discipline with discernment as a spiritual gift. How do you think these forms of discernment complement each other in navigating today's complex cultural landscape?

REFLECTION EXERCISE

Recall a time when you felt spiritually lost, disoriented, or uncertain about what God was doing. Write that story out in a journal. Where were you? What voices were pulling you in different directions?

Part 1

Hearing God

one

Making Sense of Secularism

One summer, I was invited to contribute to a small conference on global Christianity. The keynote speaker was a well-known scholar and educator from Ghana, and his respondent was a notable Nigerian scholar based in the States. I settled into a seat in the middle of the room, eager to discover what the Spirit was up to in Africa. The conference had already given us a lot to think about, covering topics like charismatic worship practices across the African diaspora and the shifting dynamics in African spirituality. But right then, everyone's attention was on Ghana.

The speaker delivered an engaging talk about the emerging Christian movements in his country. He pointed out that the older mission-based denominations in Ghana were falling behind the livelier Charismatic and Pentecostal congregations. According to him, a major reason for the rise of renewal movements throughout Africa is their profound experience of the Holy Spirit, which includes the practice of the so-called extravagant spiritual gifts such as tongues, healing, and prophecy. The theologian's presentation ended and the room was stirred by his wisdom and prophetic urgency.

Then came the response from the Nigerian theologian, whose theological and philosophical writings on African Christianity had shaped a generation. True to the style of academic conferences, he kicked things off with some positive remarks and highlighted key points from the earlier presentation. Only after that did he dive into his critiques—one of which caught me off guard. He said, "When we talk about spiritual gifts like speaking in tongues, we must think about *which spirit* these tongues are coming from." This struck me because the answer seemed so obvious—of course, the gift of tongues comes from the Holy Spirit! Why would anyone question that? Then it hit me: I had been viewing the gift of tongues through a Western lens, while he approached tongues from an African perspective.

In the West, we tend to be skeptical about supernatural, spiritual matters; a growing number of people don't buy into the idea of unseen spiritual forces.[1] Because the only ones in the West who seem to embrace speaking in tongues are Pentecostal and Charismatic Christians, we often associate **glossolalia** (speaking in unknown languages) with these Spirit-centric traditions. But from an African viewpoint, even non-Christians engage in similar practices.

There are various traditional African religious practices akin to glossolalia, though these behaviors carry different spiritual or cultural meanings. In many of these traditional religions, like the Yoruba religion in Nigeria and the Zulu Sangomas in South Africa, spiritual leaders or healers might enter altered states of consciousness during rituals. These states are thought to facilitate communication with ancestors, spirits, or deities, and in these moments, individuals often speak in

1. Belief in supernatural beings like angels and demons differs quite a bit across Western nations but seems to be declining across the board. For example, about 70 percent of people in the US think angels are real and around 50 percent believe in demons. In contrast, only 40–50 percent of people in Western Europe believe in angels and even fewer are convinced about demons. See Holly Meyer, "Nearly 7 in 10 U.S. Adults Believe in Angels, AP-NORC Poll Finds," PBS, July 29, 2023, https://www.pbs.org/newshour/nation/nearly-7-in-10-u-s-adults-believe-in-angels-ap-norc-poll-finds; and "Two Global Religious Divides: Geographical and Generational," Ipsos, November 5, 2023, https://www.ipsos.com/en/two-global-religious-divides-geographic-and-generational.

languages that are unfamiliar or unintelligible.[2] While this can look a lot like Christian glossolalia, it's seen as a spirit communicating through a medium rather than as a personal prayer language. Nevertheless, outside listeners hear what appears to be tongues. The Nigerian theologian at the conference thus implored us to always ask if the tongues are coming from the Spirit of Christ or from evil, unknown spirits.

While the Nigerian theologian was talking about the importance of spiritual discernment in African Christianity, his remarks also highlighted why we need to be discerning across different cultures. He urged African Christians to be aware of the spirits in their own cultural contexts, yet I found myself recognizing some major differences between my Western framework and his African perspective. This highlights the reality of our global pluralistic age—we have our own distinct cultures and traditions that exist within a wider framework of many other cultures and traditions. We can think about it as a tension between the local and the global, or what sociologists call the "glocal." **Glocality** refers to the interplay between the local and global factors that shape a person's identity. A glocal person navigates their surroundings by engaging with, critiquing, or responding to local cultures, nearby cultures, and the inevitable impact of globalization on cultural diversity.

Our current situation is best understood as glocal and pluralistic rather than secular. This chapter will try to make sense of our pluralistic era—a crucial first step for any contemporary cultural engagement. By exploring the work of Charles Taylor and considering his various concepts of secularity, this chapter will ultimately conclude that his idea of "Secularity 3" should be viewed as glocal and pluralistic. Secularity in this sense acts as a neutral ground where various religious, secular, philosophical, and political perspectives can coexist, which differs from how we usually think of "secular" as meaning "areligious." This chapter will also draw on James K. A. Smith's work to suggest that we should see everything as spiritually

2. Samuel Abogunrin, *The First Letter of Paul to the Corinthians* (Uzima, 1988), 126.

formative. As mentioned earlier, it requires discernment to figure out what kinds of spirits we're dealing with and to distinguish when our revelatory experiences are genuinely from God, especially in this age. This chapter will thus conclude with an emphasis on how crucial it is to pray continuously and cultivate an intimate relationship with Christ to truly recognize God's voice.

Is This the Worst Era Ever?

The introduction of this book described our age of pluralism as one defined by the social interactions happening in a complex global scene. One of the major challenges of recognizing God's voice today is the fact that so many voices are competing for our attention. Some voices say they have a better path for us than what God offers, others argue that we're misunderstanding what God is saying, and still others claim outright to be God themselves. Figuring out who to trust and what's actually true can be difficult. And when a million voices tell us a million different reasons their way is the best, it's hard to know what's right. Yet while our era has its own set of challenges, that doesn't mean things are tougher now than in the past. When thinking about today's hurdles, sometimes we can confuse "new" with "worse."

There was, for instance, a time when public executions were common, as a way to deter people from breaking the law. Imagine kids strolling through the streets and witnessing criminals facing horrific fates like being burned alive, decapitated, or fed to wild animals. For entertainment, crowds would gather to watch brutal fights to the death. This same period saw the buying and selling of slaves, who endured beatings, sexual abuse, and terrible working and living conditions. Infanticide was practiced too, with unwanted babies left to die in remote places—often babies with disabilities or little girls, who were seen as financial burdens on the family.[3] Women were treated

3. See chap. 2 of Thomas Martin, *Ancient Rome: From Romulus to Justinian* (Yale University Press, 2012), for a detailed account of first-century Roman values and practices.

like property, making domestic violence and marital rape all too common. Many deviant sexual practices stemmed from exploitation and power imbalances. Prostitution was not only legal but widespread and often the only way some women could make money to survive. Young boys were sexually exploited by older men. There was no age of consent. Public sexual acts were sometimes part of religious ceremonies, and the rich often threw lavish parties that turned into wild orgies.[4] Sounds pretty grim, right? This is a glimpse into the Roman Empire of the first century, the very time and place Jesus inhabited.

Every era after the fall has had and will continue to have an ugly side. Every era has been marred by sin, and they all had their own unique ways of instituting evil. Evil has been around since Eden and will continue until Christ comes back and sets everything right. If we zoom out globally and consider some of the worst atrocities from just the last century, the list is staggering: the Armenian genocide of the 1910s; Stalin's Holodomor famine of the early 1930s; the Holocaust of the 1940s; racialized violence during the Civil Rights Movement of the 1950s and '60s; the chemical warfare of the Vietnam War from the 1950s to the 1970s; the Tiananmen Square massacre of 1989; the Rwandan genocide of 1994; the wave of global terrorist attacks throughout the 2000s; and the ongoing refugee crisis that forces millions to escape violence, war, and environmental issues, especially in regions like the Middle East, Africa, and South Asia. This is just a snapshot of the last 110 years, but if we dig deeper into history, we can find countless instances of famines, wars, genocides, natural disasters, and oppressive regimes. In every era, society's most pressing concerns shift depending on the circumstances, and in every era, Christians have had to learn what it means to embody Christ for others. Today is no different. Our current challenges are difficult in new but not necessarily worse ways.

We should trust that God didn't put us on this planet in these times by accident. Whatever challenges this era brings, the Spirit equips

4. For an explanation of how Romans discussed matters of sexual taboo in their society, see Catherine Edwards, *The Politics of Immorality in Ancient Rome* (Cambridge University Press, 1993).

and empowers us to be Christ's witnesses. Our task, therefore, is to recognize God's voice and discern what God is doing in our world today. As William Barry says, "The wisdom necessary for discernment requires an acceptance of the present environment as the one and only theatre for my action."[5] In other words, God's calling on our lives is meant to be carried out in the present environment. We need to face reality for what it is, not how we wish it could be; instead of longing for the "good ol' days," let's appreciate the significance of the here and now. We must be truthful about our positionality, our history, our experiences, and the things we hope for today.[6] This allows us to get a strong sense of the historical genealogy that defines our present era.

How Secular Are We Really?

A few years ago, I had the chance to grab lunch with Canadian philosopher Charles Taylor, who's considered one of the top cultural theorists of our time. His work spans multiple disciplines, blending philosophy, sociology, history, and political theory. In his most influential book, *A Secular Age*, he dives deep into the history and philosophy of secularism, challenging the notion that secularism causes a decline in religious belief. This book has become a modern classic and is often seen as one of the best examinations of Western secularism today. So, how did I end up having lunch with someone like him?

In 2017, Taylor was a keynote speaker at an academic conference I regularly attend. My friend, an amazing scholar and mentor, hosted a panel featuring Taylor, and after the talk, my friend was asked if some young scholars would like to join him and Taylor for lunch. He invited me and a few others to join. During the meal, we talked about topics ranging from the church and society to hockey. We picked his brain about his groundbreaking ideas and gained insights into what

5. William Barry, "Toward a Theology of Discernment," *The Way Supplement* 64 (1989): 138.

6. Gordon Smith, *The Voice of Jesus: Discernment, Prayer and the Witness of the Spirit* (IVP, 2003), 21.

our secular age means and how it relates to pluralism. I learned a lot from Taylor at that lunch and from reading through his work. So as we look to understand our present age, let's start by considering what Taylor has to say.

In *A Secular Age*, Taylor aims to highlight the "conditions of belief" that distinguish our current time from earlier prehumanist and modernist periods.[7] The key question fueling his work is how a nonreligious perspective has become a legitimate choice today—something that would have seemed impossible even five hundred years ago. Essentially, Taylor wants to uncover the factors that transformed a theocentric (God-centered) Western society into a secular one. How did we transition into this secular age? Taylor tackles this by breaking down the term "secular" into three distinct meanings.

Secularity 1: A Premodern Sense of the Secular

Taylor calls the first sense of secularism **Secularity 1**, which refers to the separation of religion and public institutions.[8] The idea of "the secular" originates from Latin medieval Christendom, as ordinary time or space. "Secular," in this sense, is used in a straightforward, descriptive way. In the Secularity 1 framework, a secular job, for example, could be something like working as a postman or bank clerk, whereas a sacred job would be working as a priest or missionary. This distinction separates domains. However, Secularity 1 goes further than the medieval concept of secularism by separating out society's fundamental orientation, which began creating a "secular default" for public spaces. In the medieval era, even though there was a clear descriptive difference between secular and sacred, God was still seen as ever-present at secular jobs.[9] While Secularity 1 saw the existence of a secularized public space,[10] the idea of God was always a fundamental aspect of a person's reality.

7. Charles Taylor, *A Secular Age* (Harvard University Press, 2007), 28.
8. Taylor, *Secular Age*, 1.
9. Taylor, *Secular Age*, 2.
10. Taylor, *Secular Age*, 20.

To understand Secularity 1, let's try a little thought experiment. Picture a young baker in medieval England who falls seriously ill. He's a baker, so his job is secular, but his illness seems somehow divinely orchestrated. What might the locals think caused his sickness? One person might suggest that the baker should reflect on his recent behavior and repent, believing the illness is a punishment from above. Another could say that God sent the sickness to test the baker's faith. Someone else might claim it's the work of demons and urge the baker to find an exorcist. A medieval physician could argue that the baker is suffering from "miasma," or bad air, which signals God's discontent with the town. Yet still another may suspect a witch has put a curse on the baker. Since no one can figure out what's going on, the townsfolk decide the illness is part of God's mysterious plan. The baker's friends and neighbors see the world through a lens where God is in charge of everything, but they also believe that demons and spirits can influence their daily lives. Everything has a purpose, and even science is ultimately subject to a divine will. This is the sort of social imaginary that drove the medieval mind. Taylor describes a **social imaginary** as the way individuals perceive their social lives, how they connect with others, the dynamics of their interactions, the expectations they have, and the deeper values that shape those expectations.[11]

Secularity 2: A Modern Sense of the Secular

Taylor's second sense of secularity, known as **Secularity 2**, refers to the decline of religious belief and practice in society. While Secularity 1 focused on the constant presence of God and used the term "secular" mainly to differentiate between sacred and secular roles, Secularity 2 highlighted a person or institution's complete lack of religious affiliation. Essentially, this drop in religious beliefs and practices led to some people in society being labeled "areligious" or "secular." This concept came from the Enlightenment's push for

11. Charles Taylor, *Modern Social Imaginaries* (Duke University Press, 2004), 23.

disenchantment—the idea that the West shifted from a world filled with spirits and the supernatural to one driven by rational thought.[12]

Let's revisit our sick baker, but this time, let's jump ahead to Enlightenment England. What would his friends and family think about his illness now? The baker has a mix of secular agnostic and Christian friends. His agnostic buddies might lean on science, suggesting that maybe the food or water he's been consuming is tainted. Some could recommend he take a closer look at his diet and nutrition, while others might think he's just burned out or too tired. The physician still believes it's miasma and advises the baker to improve the ventilation in his room. In contrast, one of the baker's Christian friends might argue that this is divine providence and that God is teaching the baker patience. Another might see the illness as nudging the baker to renew his faith and be more committed to the church. One person even suggests that the illness could be God's way of purging the baker of spiritual impurities as a pathway to his redemption. Unlike the medieval Christians who saw divine action wrapped up in a world of spirits, the Enlightenment Christians tend to think of the baker's illness in terms of God's willed action for his life. Yet many of the baker's secular friends view the Christians as superstitious, and the Christians see the secular folks as too worldly. Maybe the baker has one open-minded Christian friend who thinks he should balance faith and reason by seeking medical help while also praying for healing, but the baker recognizes that this balanced approach is a bit out of the norm for his day and age.

In Secularity 2, there's a clear divide between faith and reason, fueled by a mutual distrust of each side. Philosopher James K. A. Smith notes that theories of secularization are usually talking about Secularity 2, suggesting that society will keep moving away from religion.[13] However, Taylor argues that our current situation isn't Secularity 2 but a new concept: Secularity 3.

12. Taylor, *Secular Age*, 15.

13. James K. A. Smith, *How (Not) to Be Secular: Reading Charles Taylor* (Eerdmans, 2014), 21.

Secularity 3: Our Current Sense of the Secular

Secularity 3 views secularity as one legitimate option among many in a pluralistic society. This sense of secularity represents a total change in the West's social imaginary. In medieval times, the Western social imaginary had three key elements: (1) The natural world was seen as a reflection of divine will, with events like floods and plagues viewed as acts of God; (2) society was intertwined with the divine, meaning kings and their realms were seen as part of a heavenly order; and (3) the world was enchanted, inhabited by spirits, demons, and moral guiding forces that people believed influenced their lives.[14] The modern social imaginary of Secularity 3 pushes back against these ideas. For Taylor, Secularity 3 isn't just a departure from a God-centered view of Secularity 1 (which is essentially what Secularity 2 was); it's about the new secular reality we navigate today. In other words, this secular age introduces new conditions of belief that shape the experiences of everyone in society, regardless of their personal faith.

Taylor highlights five traits of the modern social imaginary of Secularity 3. First, the rational and disenchanted West has given rise to what he terms the **buffered self**, marked by a strong sense of independence and self-sufficiency. Buffered people see themselves as impenetrable from outside spiritual influences, like how water rolls off of a freshly waxed car. Rather than relying on an external spiritual world, a buffered person's identity and power comes from within. In contrast, the medieval social imaginary is best viewed as porous, where the line between the mind and the world is blurry. Instead of waxed cars, medieval people were like sponges that absorb water. Back then, an enchanted perspective helped explain natural events as people "soaked up" external spiritual influences.[15] With Secularity 3, however, we have a more bounded imaginary—the outside world feels separate from our minds.[16] Smith adds that it wasn't just about

14. Taylor, *Secular Age*, 25–26.
15. Taylor, *Secular Age*, 35.
16. Taylor, *Secular Age*, 37–38.

getting rid of angels and demons; it was crucial for the self to be buffered and shielded.[17] This shift in meaning, and the buffering of the self, helped clear the way for disbelief.

Second, the buffered self lets people take a step back and focus on their own experiences, which leads to a more exclusive humanism.[18] Human flourishing turned into a personal journey centered around hard work and resourcefulness. On the other hand, the porous world of the Middle Ages made it easy for people to connect with each other. The social events and rituals in an enchanted world fostered feelings of unity, like "we're all in this together."[19] Think about the festivals that were celebrated during the harvest season of an agricultural cycle. They often carried a sense of cosmic significance because the harvest was believed to be dependent on divine forces. The community feasted, danced, played games, and gave offerings together to ensure a bountiful crop.

Third, Secularity 3 challenges the medieval idea of an "equilibrium in tension" when it comes to human flourishing on earth versus the hope for eternal life.[20] People today let go of the heavy expectations of eternity that weigh down their everyday lives. Instead, they see ultimate flourishing as something that happens right here in this world.[21] This perspective shakes up the medieval belief that some higher power is controlling every detail of existence.

Fourth, the medieval imagination had an idea of a higher, heavenly time that existed outside of our regular, linear timeline. This higher time rearranged earthly events, making it possible for things that seem distant in our world to be closely connected in the divine realm. Today, though, people tend to ignore this concept of higher time and focus solely on the current natural order of things.

Fifth, the medieval imagination viewed the cosmos as a divinely organized system, while the modern viewpoint sees it only as a huge

17. J. Smith, *How (Not) to Be Secular*, 30.
18. Taylor, *Secular Age*, 42.
19. Taylor, *Secular Age*, 42.
20. Taylor, *Secular Age*, 44.
21. J. Smith, *How (Not) to Be Secular*, 33.

expanse governed by natural laws.[22] Today a modern mind *could* think natural laws are governed by God, like Christians and other religious folks do, or they could think that natural laws are self-governed, like nonreligious folks do. The point is, Secularity 3 accounts for an era where a nonreligious worldview has become a legitimate choice.

The **immanent frame** we find ourselves in is a secular worldview that emphasizes the material and observable elements of reality, steering clear of references to higher or divine dimensions. What Taylor is getting at is that today we have a buffered identity in a secular world that exists within a framework that sets up a "natural" order, contrasting it with a "supernatural" one. Thus the immanent frame can be juxtaposed with the transcendent frame of the Middle Ages.[23]

Yet we shouldn't strive to retreat back to a medieval transcendent frame—science and empiricism have forever changed the way we view reality. Rather, Christians should think about how God engages us in an immanent frame. What does it mean to believe in God's divine action today? Smith says, "The question isn't whether we inhabit the immanent frame, but how. Some inhabit it as a closed frame with a brass ceiling; others inhabit it as an open frame with skylights open to transcendence."[24] Smith (reading Taylor) suggests that Christians should embrace an open frame that acknowledges the current situation while still holding on to hope for transcendence, for God to break through.

I've witnessed many pastors and teachers give lackluster accounts of secularism—they often paint hopeless pictures of Secularity 2 and argue that we should double down on our convictions in the face of a godless secular society. Doubling down for these pastors often means breakdowns in dialogue and empathy toward others. But we live in a condition of secularity that sees religious and nonreligious ideologies existing side by side. In other words, not everyone is godless. In fact, most people hold to some sort of faith. Our task in Secularity 3 should thus be more like Paul's when he stands in the midst of the

22. Taylor, *Secular Age*, 60.
23. Taylor, *Secular Age*, 542.
24. J. Smith, *How (Not) to Be Secular*, 93.

Areopagus in Acts 17:22–23: He commends the Athenians for their faith and religious fervor but demonstrates how they have put their faith in the wrong thing. As Christians, our witness in Secularity 3 should constitute a different sort of apologetics. We don't need to prove the legitimacy of our faith tradition, because faith traditions are already viewed favorably or at least tolerably. Instead, we need to prove that our tradition is the best option. We need to show why our faith is true rather than false, good rather than corrupt, and beautiful rather than vile.

Secularity in Global Context

Taylor's concepts of Secularity 3 and the immanent frame offer us a deeper understanding of our current circumstances in the West. However, I think Taylor somewhat overlooks a significant outcome of this change in belief systems: the West's return to a global perspective. From the beginning of his work, Taylor admits that he's focusing on the origins of secularity in the West. While he doesn't propose a global analysis of secularization, he does believe that such a study is needed. He writes, "It should be possible some day to undertake a study of the whole phenomenon on a global scale. But I don't think one can start there. This is because secularity, like other features of 'modernity,' . . . find rather different expression, and develop under the pressure of different demands and aspirations in different civilizations."[25] Our experience of modernity isn't just one-size-fits-all; Taylor says we actually live in a global reality that showcases many forms of modernity.[26] Because of this, mapping out all the ways secularity shows up in these "multiple modernities" would be a challenge.

Still, that's not my main issue with Taylor's viewpoint. What's overlooked is the fact that the West has reconnected with the global community, largely due to the impact of Secularity 3. Essentially, Secularity 3 does more than just allow religious and nonreligious

25. Taylor, *Secular Age*, 20.
26. Taylor, *Modern Social Imaginaries*, 1–2.

beliefs to coexist; it promotes a deep sense of tolerance that's necessary for forming *glocal* understandings of the world. In fact, I brought this point up to Taylor at our lunch, and he agreed.

In this age of pluralism, Western folks are curious about other cultures and believe that different perspectives have their own value. There's been a shift: The West now sees its own way of life as just one option among many in a bigger global community. Perhaps Taylor overlooked how these changes have influenced the West's self-perception through interactions with the rest of the world. Secularity 3 has turned into a platform where Western and non-Western belief systems can encounter each other—and even transform each other. This is what it means to say we've entered what Smith calls a "globalized, cosmopolitan, pluralist present."[27]

Another way to describe our present is through the concept of glocality. The word "glocal" first popped up in the late 1980s as a business term to talk about "global localization,"[28] referring to how global brands adapt to fit local markets. Over time, the word has evolved to mean something broader. It now refers to situations and realities that take both local and global factors into account. Today, more local viewpoints are entering the global conversation, and globalization is also shaping local discussions.

Victor Roudometof describes glocalization as "globalization refracted through the local."[29] Global influences pass through local cultures like light that travels through a prism, creating a spectrum of differences that result in glocal refractions.[30] Globalization doesn't completely erase cultural uniqueness but repackages the cultural product into many glocal expressions.[31] The glocal viewpoint is positioned

27. J. Smith, *How (Not) to Be Secular*, x.

28. Victor Roudometof, *Glocalization: A Critical Introduction* (Routledge, 2016), 2.

29. Roudometof, *Glocalization*, 64.

30. Roudometof, *Glocalization*, 64.

31. If you think of the local perspective as being on the edge of a community looking inward, you might assume the global perspective is also positioned at the edge of the world looking in. However, both assumptions miss the mark. The local viewpoint is narrow and often ignores the interconnected and international aspects of our current reality. Conversely, the idea of a global viewpoint is actually impossible. No one can truly step outside of all local contexts to observe a perfect, unbiased

at the heart of a community, looking outward to the global, already filtered and interpreted through local experiences. It acknowledges its local roots while recognizing that its specific situation is part of a larger, more complete picture.

So what kind of advice is our English baker getting today? Let's assume he lives in a diverse area of London and has all sorts of friends. His Christian buddy thinks his illness is a cue to pray for healing and trust in God. Meanwhile, his Muslim friend recommends giving to charity, believing that it will bring blessings and healing from God. Scrolling through social media, the baker catches a video of a Buddhist who suggests he embrace illness with mindfulness and find balance in both body and mind. Then his scientifically minded STEM professor points to germs, viruses, or bacteria as the culprits to his illness and advises him to improve his hygiene and see a doctor. His therapist thinks he should focus on rest and try some stress management techniques, suggesting that his sickness might be tied to stress or being overworked. Last, one of his New Age friends claims his energy is off and that he should try Reiki. There are so many viewpoints that our baker friend feels overwhelmed. He decides to just go to the doctor and take some medicine.

When we compare the three bakers across time, we notice that they are all thinking through their illnesses in very different ways. The medieval baker (Secularity 1) is given a lot of advice, but it all seems to point back to divine action. The Enlightenment baker (Secularity 2) is given both religious advice and scientific advice and feels like he must deny one to find his answer. Finally, the contemporary baker (Secularity 3) is given a plethora of religious, pseudo-religious, scientific, and pseudo-scientific advice from all over the world. As he wades through the various perspectives, he defaults to naturalism

perspective on something, as that would overlook their own geographical and communal ties. Nermin Saybasili points out that "the processes of globalization are the phenomenon of abstraction. However, what is global, that operates 'nowhere,' is always localized; it always inhabits a 'now-here.'" Nermin Saybasili, "Gesturing No(w)here," in *Globalization and Contemporary Art*, ed. Jonathan Harris (Wiley-Blackwell, 2011), 410.

since he's still in an immanent frame. We shouldn't think that any of the bakers ever had it easy; they each had to overcome various challenges. Using these categories, we can see that Taylor is helpful for clarifying what secularity means in our Western perspective. He effectively highlights how our current situation is different from the post-Enlightenment modern era. This framework gives us a glimpse into our future by mapping out a thorough history of what has come before.

Recognizing God's Voice Amid Various Spiritualities

Since many religious, secular, philosophical, and political perspectives coexist in our pluralist present, our task is to discern between the spirits of our age. When we think about these various perspectives, we have to ask, Which spirit are these tongues coming from? While Secularity 1 and 2 distinguished between the secular and the sacred, could one of the shifts of Secularity 3 be that we recognize everything as, in some way, spiritually formative? Could we, for instance, think of areligious worldview formations as modes of spiritual formation or malformation? This idea appears to be subtly reflected in the comments made by the Nigerian theologian at the beginning of this chapter. But in what ways can secular worldviews then form (or deform) us spiritually?

What Else Is Forming Us?

It's not too difficult to see how other religious worldviews form people. Take Buddhism, for example; its rituals and teachings guide people toward a Buddhist spirituality. The same goes for Islam, where its practices and teachings lead people to embrace a Muslim spirituality. Similarly, a blend of pseudo-religious practices from mysticism, self-help, wellness trends, and esoteric beliefs shape a loosely defined, individualistic New Age spirituality. It's a bit trickier, however, to see how secular practices shape us and to understand the kinds of spiritualities that come from them.

James K. A. Smith offers an insightful perspective on how a secular worldview can spiritually form us. In his book *Desiring the Kingdom*, Smith explores the question of what defines our humanity. The Enlightenment concept of humanity was that we are primarily thinking beings (*homo sapiens* etymologically means "rational human"). But what about our physical bodies, our feelings, and our emotions? Aren't those just as crucial in shaping who we are and vital to our human existence? We shouldn't only see ourselves as thinking beings; we should also recognize that we are desiring beings who experience the world bodily, emotionally, and intellectually.[32] Smith ultimately concludes that our loves and desires are what motivate our actions: "What we desire or love ultimately is a (largely implicit) vision of what we hope for, what we think the good life looks like. This vision of the good life shapes all kinds of actions and decisions and habits that we undertake, often without our thinking about it."[33] The mind is central to who we are, but it's not the only aspect of our being. Our actions are determined by the things we ultimately put our hope in.

Smith suggests we are "liturgical animals" because our habits, rituals, and embodied practices shape us more than just our abstract thoughts and reason.[34] When he speaks of **liturgy**, he's not only referring to practices in religious services; he's including any repeated, formative practices that guide our hearts toward a vision of the good life. A liturgy, therefore, consists of the daily rituals that influence our desires.[35] This can mean a traditional church service but also repeated secular practices like shopping, watching sports, or spending time on social media—what we can call **secular liturgy**. Our lives are packed with these cultural liturgies (both sacred and secular) that shape us in ways we might not even notice. Myriad cultural practices, faith-based or otherwise, are vying for our attention and, ultimately, our desires.

32. James K. A. Smith, *Desiring the Kingdom: Worship, Worldview, and Cultural Formation* (Baker Academic, 2009), 24.
33. J. Smith, *Desiring the Kingdom*, 27.
34. J. Smith, *Desiring the Kingdom*, 40.
35. J. Smith, *Desiring the Kingdom*, 35.

Smith believes that since we are holistic beings, our emotions and senses play a huge role in shaping who we are. He sees embodied practices as essential for our spiritual formation. Think about a basketball coach who notices a player struggling with their shooting form. The coach might have them take shots close to the basket using just one arm. He'll tell them to concentrate on the angle of their arm, how they extend it, and how they follow through with their wrists. He'll make them repeat this hundreds of times until it becomes second nature. Then during a game, the hooper can rely on muscle memory instead of stressing about his shooting form. Similarly, we can develop spiritually by consistently participating in liturgical practices. Fasting, praying, reading the Bible, and worshiping together help mold our spiritual lives and build what we could call our spiritual muscle memory.

We can think of a **secular spirituality**[36] as a holistic outlook of the world that comes from being formed areligiously in today's immanent frame. What might that look like in our Western context? As I've mentioned elsewhere, liberalism is a key feature of our society. When I talk about liberalism, I'm not referring to partisan politics but to the Enlightenment concept of liberalism, which focuses on personal freedom, equality, and individual rights.[37] In our society, liberalism creates its own kind of spirituality, where individualism and

36. Theologian James Cone expresses a similar idea about nonreligious yet spiritual musical expressions in Black music. He refers to Black music as "unity music," which connects communities through shared feelings of joy, sorrow, love, hate, hope, and despair (James Cone, *The Spirituals and the Blues: An Interpretation* [Orbis Books, 1991], 5). This music is all about liberation and is deeply affirming and communal, reflecting the collective struggles of Black Americans. As Cone states, "The basic idea of the spirituals is that slavery contradicts God; it is a denial of God's will. To be enslaved is to be declared *nobody*, and that form of existence contradicts God's creation of people to be God's children. Because black people believed that they were God's children, they affirmed their *somebodiness*, refusing to reconcile their servitude with divine revelation" (33). Cone points out that both blues and spirituals come from the same source of spiritual experience and are best appreciated together. Thus, blues can best be understood as a "secular spiritual," as a counterpoint to the sacredness of the Black spiritual (98).

37. Steven Félix-Jäger, *The Problem and Promise of Freedom: A Public Theology for the Church* (Baker Academic, 2025), 2.

democratic governance shape our perspective of the world through ideals like freedom, industriousness, fairness, and diversity.[38] When we think about the phrase "pull yourself up by your bootstraps," for example, we think of Western industriousness and self-reliance. We think of self-made success. We confess that with enough grit and determination, anyone can achieve their goals, no matter where they come from or what challenges they face. We think of the American Dream. For many, it's not just a saying; it's a spiritual way of being, a secular spirituality.

We could say marketization in a free-market society also forms a sort of spirituality. In a free market, it's the consumers who decide what products and services are out there based on how they spend their money. Trends are shaped by what people choose to buy; ads push people to buy what a company is selling. Marketers work hard to connect with consumers on an emotional and even spiritual level, making them feel something for the products or services advertised. Competitive markets don't just influence what we want—they also keep that desire in us alive. They thrive on creating a cycle where people are always wanting more, whether it's new products or fresh experiences. As long as we have that itch for something new, we're driven to keep buying,[39] trapped in a secular spirituality based on consumption.

There are many more things we could point to as secular spiritualities (e.g., sports fandoms, music and festival culture, eco-activism, pop-culture fandoms, and wellness culture). The point is, these ideologies, cultures, and fandoms offer ways of being that affect our whole selves. As spiritualities, they develop cultural rituals and treat their luminaries like secular saints. They form us deeply. For Smith, we thus have two choices: We can dive into a secular liturgy of self-indulgence by constantly engaging in worldly activities, or we can embrace a liturgy that draws us nearer to Christ by consistently practicing kingdom-focused actions. The secular activities are not

38. Félix-Jäger, *Problem and Promise of Freedom*, 99.
39. Félix-Jäger, *Problem and Promise of Freedom*, 63.

necessarily bad in themselves but become bad when they are given our ultimate allegiance—when they are allowed first rights to form us. This is when they cross over from being fun activities to deeply formative idols.

As discerners in a pluralistic age, our job isn't just to see that these practices are formative but to discern what kind of spiritual people they are turning us into. Spiritualities are not neutral; they bend our hearts toward a vision of reality. The real question isn't if secular rituals shape us—it's which vision of reality they are shaping us toward. Gordon Smith writes, "We must learn to distinguish, for not all 'spiritual' experience finds its source in God."[40] After all, 1 John 4:1 says to "test the spirits to see whether they are from God, for many false prophets have gone out into the world." Paul also tells us to "test everything; hold fast to what is good" (1 Thess. 5:21). The remainder of this chapter will thus look at what testing everything entails and what sort of criteria we might use to determine what genuinely comes from God.

Criteria for Discerning Our Spiritual Experiences

Discerning God's voice involves recognizing when our spiritual experiences are from God or when they are shaped by other spiritual influences. Since so many spiritualities seek our attention, recognizing God's voice requires knowing God on a deep and intimate level. Discernment and prayer go hand in hand because constant prayer allows us to recognize God's voice, to get to know God's personality, and to learn what moves God's heart. Think of it like having a crush on someone. You might check out their social media or chat with friends you both know to gather information. But to truly get to know them, you need to spend some quality time together. The same goes for Jesus—to truly know him, we need to spend time with him. And prayer is how we do that.

Prayer is essential for our spiritual formation since it helps us connect with God on a personal level, which in turn shapes who we

40. G. Smith, *Voice of Jesus*, 19.

are—our hearts, minds, and character. Praying is basically having a chat with God. We do it on our own and in community, whether we're singing songs to God or tuning in to what God is saying. In prayer, we draw near to God's presence (James 4:8). We start to reflect Christ's image, adopting facets of his character, like patience, humility, and love (2 Cor. 3:18). Prayer also guides us in understanding and accepting God's plans, steering us away from a life guided by our own carnal desires (Ps. 25:4–5). By making prayer a regular part of our lives, we shift our focus back to God's truth and seek out what accords with God's will (1 John 5:14–15). Prayer also teaches us to trust in God's timing and faithfulness (Matt. 7:7–8). Ultimately, living a prayerful life keeps us constantly aware of God's presence, turning our entire days into a constant conversation with God. Paul tells us to "pray without ceasing" (1 Thess. 5:17), and this never-ceasing lifestyle of prayer invites God into every facet of our lives. A friend of mine mentioned that he wraps up his prayers with an "Amen," but then he jumps right back in with a "Dear God . . . ," and just lets it sit there. For him, it's a way to remind himself that his chats with God are ongoing.

Getting to know God on an intimate level through prayer ultimately fosters our ability to discern. As Gordon Smith says,

> While God speaks to us in the whole of our lives and potentially within just about any circumstances and through any person who comes our way, we will not recognize the voice of Jesus unless we establish the pattern of listening to the Spirit in our prayers. We learn to listen in prayer. Then, in time, the whole of our lives will be marked by our capacity to listen. Thus mature pray-ers are those who are not just attentive to Jesus in prayer; they have over time become women and men who are able to discern the inner witness of the Spirit in the midst of life and work.[41]

But even as we constantly pray, how can we tell that we're not just talking to ourselves? How can we distinguish God's voice from our

41. G. Smith, *Voice of Jesus*, 26.

own, which has been influenced by our emotions or even other spiritualities? When we feel like we've had a revelatory experience from God, how can we tell that it's genuine?

In her insightful study, theologian Tania Harris interviewed members from three different Pentecostal churches in Australia to explore how they perceive hearing from God. She wanted to find out how they distinguish their spiritual experiences as genuine revelations from God instead of just as personal feelings or influences from other spirits. Their answers are illuminating, and I think we can use them as guidelines for our own discernment. The churchgoers cited seven criteria to test their experiences against: the Scriptures, the character of God, the emotional impact of the experience, the "otherness" of the voice, the hearing of previously unknown information, secondary revelatory experiences, and agreement from trusted friends, family members, or spiritual leaders.[42] Typically, the churchgoers relied on a combination of these factors to determine whether their experience was from God.

Testing experiences against Scripture makes a lot of sense. After all, 2 Timothy 3:16 says, "All scripture is inspired by God and is useful for teaching, for reproof, for correction, and for training in righteousness." In other words, the Bible itself says that Scripture can and should be used as a reliable standard for discernment because it's able to teach and correct us. Along with testing experiences, there's biblical precedence for testing teachings against Scripture. The book of Acts, for instance, recounts the faithfulness of the Berean Jews as they listened openly to Paul and Silas's teachings but then held those teachings up against Scripture: "They welcomed the message very eagerly and examined the scriptures every day to see whether these things were so" (Acts 17:11). Likewise, the congregants whom Harris interviewed said succinctly, "If it's from God, it should be in line with the Word of God."[43] Sometimes our experiences might not

42. Tania Harris, *Hearing God's Voice: Towards a Theology of Contemporary Pentecostal Revelatory Experience* (Brill, 2023), 167.

43. Harris, *Hearing God's Voice*, 167. We should note that while Roman Catholics also see the magisterium and tradition as officially authoritative to test experiences against, Protestants view Scripture as its most foundational authority.

be explicitly stated in the Bible. In those situations, they should still align with the overall message of Scripture and definitely shouldn't contradict anything found in it.

The congregants also mentioned "the character of God" as a criterion for discernment. This could come off as a bit circular: First, you experience God. Then, you check that experience against what you believe to be God's character, which you know from your experiences with God. But the people whom Harris talked to pointed out that understanding God's character is mainly based on Scripture. They could thus trace the source of their experience back to whether "the message was consistent with God's good and loving nature—as depicted in the Scriptures."[44]

The members of the congregation also brought up subjective criteria, like having a strong emotional response—feeling peace, hope, conviction, joy, or excitement—as a way to help confirm the authenticity of their experiences.[45] I can relate to this. There are times when I'm facing a tough decision and start to feel anxious, but then I feel an overwhelming sense of peace that seems like a gift from God, helping me brace for whatever happens. Even when I'm hopeful about something that doesn't pan out, I often feel like I had a sense of the outcome ahead of time, because God was mercifully preparing me for that disappointment. It's important to remember, though, that while criteria like this can serve as additional ways to discern experiences, they aren't definitive like Scripture is.

The members of the congregation also mentioned the "otherness of the voice" as a subjective criterion. Essentially, during prayer, they experience a distinct thought that feels like it's coming from outside themselves. These thoughts are often unexpected and not typical of what they would normally express.[46] They might also receive new information about a situation, whether it's about a person or something else, or even details about the future that haven't happened yet. Both criteria (the otherness of the voice and the hearing of new

44. Harris, *Hearing God's Voice*, 168.
45. Harris, *Hearing God's Voice*, 169.
46. Harris, *Hearing God's Voice*, 169.

information) suggest they're picking up on something externally from God during their prayers.[47]

Finally, people can seek validation of their experiences from others.[48] For example, you might feel like you're being nudged by God to return to school and finish your degree. You're praying about it, but you still feel a bit uncertain. Then, out of the blue, someone who has no prior knowledge about your prayers says, "I don't know why, but I feel like God wants you to go back to college!" The unexpected confirmation can affirm what you've been contemplating. Additionally, folks might turn to trusted family, friends, or spiritual mentors for guidance, sharing their situation to get some wise advice. This kind of counsel often functions as a criterion for discernment as well.[49] We'll likely be more assured that something is from God if a level-headed and mature Christian sees the hand of God at work in it.

These criteria aren't just relevant for our pluralistic age; they've always been essential for spiritual formation. However, in our complex and confusing world, discernment has become even more crucial, making these strategies critical. But listening for God's voice isn't enough; we must follow it. Jesus calls to us as the Good Shepherd and tells us, "My sheep hear my voice. I know them, and they follow me" (John 10:27). When we truly recognize Jesus's voice, we go where he goes. His joys become our joys, and his concerns become our concerns. As we're formed in Christ, our desires sync up, and soon our hearts start beating in unison. To sum it up, in a pluralistic age, hearing God and following the Spirit starts with one simple directive: Talk to God.

Conclusion

We need to foster a spirituality that can discern the difference between the genuine work of the Spirit and counterfeit experiences, between

47. Harris, *Hearing God's Voice*, 170.
48. Harris, *Hearing God's Voice*, 170.
49. Harris, *Hearing God's Voice*, 171.

real faith and worldly exploitations, and between God's vision and our own vanities. This discernment must be taught, cultivated, and practiced holistically in every aspect of our lives.

This chapter considered the intricacies of secularism and how Secularity 3 (our present condition in the West) presents the world as a neutral space where both religious and nonreligious views coexist. We looked at how globalization has shaped religious identities, creating a dynamic interplay between local and global influences—what we refer to as glocality. In such a context, secular beliefs and practices can develop into spiritualities of their own, which often go unnoticed. By acknowledging the spiritual aspects of secular culture, we highlighted the need for discernment to recognize God's voice amid the influences around us. While this chapter highlighted that cultivating a habit of constant prayer is the most foundational way to foster our ability to hear God's voice, the next chapter will discuss how a spiritual reading of Scripture can help us recognize God's voice amid myriad competing religious and nonreligious voices.

KEY WORDS

- **buffered self**: A conception of self that carries a strong sense of independence and self-sufficiency
- **disenchantment**: The idea that the West shifted from a world filled with spirits and the supernatural to one driven by rational thought
- **glocality**: The interplay between the local and global factors that shape a person's identity
- **glossolalia**: Speaking in unknown languages
- **immanent frame**: A secular worldview that emphasizes the material and observable elements of reality, steering clear of references to higher or divine dimensions
- **liturgy**: Any repeated, formative practices that guide our hearts toward a vision of the good life

- **secular liturgy**: Formative, repeated secular practices
- **secular spirituality**: A holistic outlook on the world that comes from being formed areligiously in an immanent frame
- **Secularity 1**: The separation of religion and public institutions
- **Secularity 2**: The decline of religious belief and practice in society
- **Secularity 3**: Regarding secularity as one legitimate option among many in a pluralistic society
- **social imaginary**: The way individuals perceive their social lives, how they connect with others, the dynamics of their interactions, the expectations they have, and the deeper values that shape those expectations

DISCUSSION QUESTIONS

- Do you agree with the claim that every era faces unique challenges but that none is inherently more difficult than others? Why or why not?
- Differentiate between Secularity 1, Secularity 2, and Secularity 3. Have you noticed people talking about secularism as if it is Secularity 2 rather than Secularity 3?
- Do you agree with all the criteria used to determine the authenticity of a divine experience? Are there any criteria you would add to the list?

REFLECTION EXERCISE

For one week, write down moments where you encounter ideas or values that claim some form of "truth" (e.g., slogans, ads, conversations). For each, ask: *What spirit is behind this? Is this shaping me toward Christ or away from him?*

two

Hearing God in the Crowded Space of Competing Narratives

A familiar voice can cut through the noise and stop us in our tracks. I'm reminded of when my daughter, Mila, was born. After many hours of labor, she finally arrived, and let me tell you, she was not happy about it. She was furious! She protested the sudden cold, the bright lights, the hurried chatter from the nurses and her doctor, and the overwhelming newness of it all. She cried with every ounce of strength her tiny lungs could muster. Can we really blame her? She did, after all, experience the world for the first time. That's a lot to take in.

The nurses wrapped her up in warm blankets and gently handed her to my wife, who was exhausted from the labor but relieved. But Mila kept crying. Her eyebrows were furrowed, and her face was scrunched up into a perfect ball of fire and confusion. The doctor took Mila to the warming bed and checked her. She was healthy, pink, and strong. Just really mad. It was at the warming station that I first met her. The doctor lifted her up like Rafiki holding up baby Simba. Then, in a soft voice, I said, "Hey, Mila." The moment Mila heard my voice, she stopped crying, opened her eyes, and looked at me. Her face, just seconds removed from being red and wrathful, now softened with curiosity. She blinked up at me as if she was trying to remember something. My heart skipped a beat. I was the first person she ever saw, and the comfort of my voice made her stop crying.

During the many months she had spent in her mother's womb, I had talked to her. I'd lean down and say hello, letting her know how excited I was to finally meet her. So when she was born and everything around her got too loud, too bright, too crazy—and all she could do was cry—the second she heard my voice again, she felt safe. The world was still big and strange, but for Mila, my voice brought her home.

Just as Mila felt scared and disoriented when she had to face so many new things at once, we too are confronted by a multitude of voices in this age of global pluralism. Bright lights and diverging conversations are everywhere, and traveling through those frequencies are countless stories and varied perspectives on life and faith. In a pluralistic world, it's easy to get confused when we hear echoes of truth in other narratives and see beauty in different traditions. We might even start to doubt: What if my faith claim is just one valid perspective among many? How do we discern God's voice amid these competing and often compelling narratives?

This chapter will explore what it means to affirm a particular faith in a world full of different beliefs. What sets *our* faith tradition apart? We'll discover that Christianity doesn't (or shouldn't) lead us back to a rigid ideology but to a person—Jesus Christ. To affirm our faith in today's pluralistic society means recognizing the particularity of Christ in the world and confessing his lordship. Since God is triune, the Spirit is constantly working in the world to reveal Christ. Jesus told his disciples, "When the Spirit of truth comes, he will guide you into all the truth, for he will not speak on his own but will speak whatever he hears, and he will declare to you the things that are to come. He will glorify me because he will take what is mine and declare it to you" (John 16:13–14). The Spirit, active everywhere, shares what's heard from the Father and reveals to us what's been entrusted to Christ—the truth—and calls us back to the *particular Christ*, the one who became flesh and was tasked with our redemption.

We still need to consider how Christ's story can stand out among so many others. Just like my voice was a guiding light for Mila when she was in her mom's womb, we must internalize Christ's voice and his story so we can recognize it, hear it, and be guided by it through all the noise. One way to find our spiritual footing is by reading Scripture in a way that's reflective and soaked in prayer. With that in mind, this chapter will wrap up with a discussion of the formative practice of spiritual reading.

A Particular Faith in a Pluralist World

As discussed in the last chapter, technology, international travel, and global communications have opened up the chance for us to engage with a variety of glocal perspectives in global dialogue. We come across a wide range of religious and cultural identities everywhere we go. Many of these socioreligious identities are beautiful, and when we see expressions of love and wisdom blossoming outside our own faith tradition, we might begin to question if our path is really the only way to God, truth, or salvation. We might begin to wonder if our view of God is too limited. Is God particular or cosmic and universal? If God is somehow all of this (a claim I'll defend later in this chapter), does that mean other religions have legitimate claims to salvific truths? Are our claims to particularity like trying to fence off an ocean? Because many voices are saying different things *about* God, discernment is needed to hear about God *from* God and to distinguish between the spirits of our age.

When religious traditions are set side by side, our own faith tradition can seem like a delicate vase in a jam-packed antique store. Should we wrap it in bubble wrap? Showcase it behind glass? Or let people handle it and risk it getting mishandled and broken? Having a particular faith means declaring, "This isn't just another thing in my collection; this is my *prized* possession." Yet we don't want to be so exclusive that we overlook or deny the humanity of others. As Christians, we believe that every person is created in the image of God, no matter their religion or cultural background (Gen. 1:26–27). We understand that God's compassion extends beyond us, embracing all people and all of creation (Ps. 145:9). We should be like trees that are firmly planted in our own soil yet have branches that extend over nearby fences. We should let our faith be our home without making others feel unhoused.

Is Religious Pluralism a Viable Option?

What should our relationship with other religions be? Some argue that all religions reflect the same ultimate reality but that different religious traditions receive and experience this universal presence through their own cultural lenses.[1] This is called **religious pluralism**, and the best-known proponent of this view is the late theologian and philosopher John Hick. Hick argues that the "Eternal One" (Hick's interreligious term for God) is "perceived within different human cultures under different forms, both personal and nonpersonal, and that from these different perceptions arise the religious ways of life which we call the great world faiths."[2] In other words, according to Hick, people from every walk encounter God and then project their own cultural backgrounds and upbringings to interpret and name God.[3] He says "the thing known is known according to the mode of the knower,"[4] which means that the manner in which people come to know God is bound up by their own human culture and history. He says all the major religions have legitimate claims to knowledge about God, but their understandings are limited and incomplete. What they know is not God in God's fullness but a divine "persona," face, or image of the Eternal One.[5] For Jews, this persona is Yahweh.

1. Alan Race, *Thinking About Religious Pluralism: Shaping Theology of Religions for Our Times* (Fortress, 2015), 40.
2. John Hick, *God Has Many Names* (Westminster, 1982), 59.
3. Hick, *God Has Many Names*, 45.
4. Hick, *God Has Many Names*, 51.
5. Hick, *God Has Many Names*, 52.

For Christians, it is Yahweh made flesh in Christ, and for Eastern religions, this persona may be Shiva or Krishna.[6] Hence, God, as the Eternal One, has many names.

In order for Hick to make these claims from a Christian vantage point, he has to make a few unorthodox moves. First, Hick recognizes that a literal reading of the incarnation would pose a major problem for pluralism: "If Jesus was literally God incarnate, the second Person of the holy Trinity living a human life, so that the Christian religion was founded by God-on-earth in person, it is then very hard to escape from the traditional view that all mankind must be converted to the Christian faith."[7] He understands that the Christian claim of the incarnation as a metaphysical truth makes Christian pluralism unfeasible, if not impossible, since the incarnation asserts that God became flesh in a single man and that it is through the death and resurrection of that man that salvation is possible. For Hick, the only way out of this debacle is to understand the incarnation metaphorically as a religious myth rather than as a metaphysical truth—a "poetic expression of the Christian's devotion to his Lord."[8] Salvation is then reinterpreted as human transformation from alienation to a better state of harmony with reality.[9]

Hick then develops a theology of religions that is not Jesus-centered or Christianity-centered but a "God-centered model of the universe of faiths."[10] In other words, he de-particularizes his theology of religion in order to make it a big-tent theology that can accommodate any religious concept of the divine. Finally, rather than calling God "God," he refers to God as the "Eternal One" of "infinite Reality" that exceeds human concepts.[11] Sometimes Hick refers to God simply as the "Real."[12]

6. Hick, *God Has Many Names*, 53.
7. Hick, *God Has Many Names*, 19.
8. Hick, *God Has Many Names*, 19.
9. John Hick, *An Interpretation of Religion: Human Responses to the Transcendent*, 2nd ed. (Palgrave Macmillan, 2004), 10.
10. Hick, *God Has Many Names*, 18.
11. Hick, *God Has Many Names*, 24.
12. Hick, *Interpretation of Religion*, xix.

I appreciate Hick's sincere attempt to reframe Christianity in light of global pluralism, but I find his conclusions problematic. Let's go ahead and name the elephant in the room: Hick has formulated a religious framework that, if it was called "Christian," would be rejected as heresy by most Christians today and throughout history. Christians bear their name because they view Jesus as God incarnate—metaphysically, not merely metaphorically. This is recorded throughout the New Testament and is later ratified in the ecumenical creeds.

One might argue that Jesus's divinity was a later addition to the faith, like a legend being formed throughout the centuries, but that's not true. The earliest texts of the New Testament, Paul's letters, were penned in the late 40s and 50s CE, a little over a decade after the death and resurrection of Jesus. The oldest of Paul's letters are likely 1 Thessalonians, Galatians, 1 and 2 Corinthians, and Romans, and they clearly demonstrate that Jesus is truly God incarnate and that salvation only comes through Christ. It is in these letters that Paul calls Jesus "the Christ, who is over all, God blessed forever" (Rom. 9:5). It is in these letters that Paul says it is through Christ that we even exist: "There is one God, the Father, from whom are all things and for whom we exist, and one Lord, Jesus Christ, through whom are all things and through whom we exist" (1 Cor. 8:6). It is in these letters that Paul talks about Jesus as our way of salvation: "If you confess with your mouth that Jesus is Lord and believe in your heart that God raised him from the dead, you will be saved" (Rom. 10:9).

These passages are all from the earliest Christian texts and written by one of the early church's main voices, indicating that the earliest churches believed Jesus to be God metaphysically, not just metaphorically. Hick's views reject Christian tradition and the foundational claims of the faith as recorded in the New Testament. Religious pluralism is thus not an orthodox Christian position. But is it even a viable *religious* position?

Speaking of elephants in rooms, a well-known image of religious pluralism is the parable of the blind men and the elephant. In this story, six blind men are brought into a room with a massive elephant, an animal none of them have ever encountered before, and they are asked to reach out and describe what they feel. The first man touches the elephant's leg and says, "Ah! This creature is like a pillar." The second man feels the ear and states, "No, this animal is like a big fan." The third man grabs the tail and shouts, "You're all wrong! This animal is like a rope." Then the fourth man brushes against its side and declares, "It's like a wall!" The fifth man holds the trunk and says, "This animal is like a snake." Finally, the sixth man touches the tusk and remarks, "You're all crazy! It's hard and smooth like a spear." Each of them is partially correct yet completely limited in their perspective. They all experience the same elephant but from different positions, which determines what part of the elephant they touch.

Similarly, religious pluralists believe that various religions engage with the same ultimate reality, each from their own perspective. Their interpretations vary not because they're wrong but because God is too vast to be fully understood by any single tradition. Depending on their faith perspective, they might see God as strong and foundational (a leg), cool and gracious (an ear), flexible yet sturdy (a tail), vast and unmovable (the side), alive and clever (the snake), or as a tool for vengeance (the tusk).

Theologian Alan Race highlights a common criticism of this parable, which is that it presupposes an all-knowing host present in the room with the blind men. If the blind men accidently stumble into the room and decide to describe the elephant, how can they possibly know that they are all touching the same animal? Race writes, "There can be no confirmation that each is touching the elephant if there is no agent external to the scene, and the absence of an external agent reflects what is the case in real life."[13] Just as a host needs to be able to see the blind men all touching the same elephant, someone has to have knowledge beyond the limited frame of their own religious (or nonreligious) tradition in order to even make the claim that they're all experiencing the same ultimate reality from different vantage points. Does John Hick have this point of view, like Superman flying above the earth's orbit to look at the whole world from

13. Race, *Thinking About Religious Pluralism*, 42.

a greater perspective? I don't think so. This critique highlights the epistemological difficulties of Hick's claims.

Even though religious pluralism aims for harmony through mutual respect and the validation of various religious traditions, many religions assert that they alone provide the path to salvation. They make, in other words, their own exclusive salvific claims. Ironically, religious pluralism becomes its own belief system that then conflicts with the very groups it intends to embrace.

As mentioned, a fundamental claim of Christianity is that salvation is possible in Christ alone. Not only do other religions disagree with this point; they even define salvation differently. Race summarizes this objection well: "It is not possible to tell whether or not another tradition is salvific, for criteria to this effect are not available outside the Christian tradition itself. 'Salvation' is a Christian category and ought not to be conflated with the cognates from other traditions, such as nirvana (Buddhism) or liberation from *moksa* (Hinduism)."[14] While most religious concepts of salvation have to do with liberation, they might entail liberation from strife, desire, or suffering. Some might view salvation as gaining rewards like paradise or union with a deity. But for Christians, **salvation** means being delivered from sin and death through Jesus's sacrifice and receiving life everlasting in a restored relationship with God. Understanding the subtle differences between these concepts of salvation is key to grasping what makes each religion unique.

For theologians like George Lindbeck, the Christian concept of salvation can only be understood contextually as part of the broader Christian narrative. Lindbeck argues that religions each have their own frameworks of interpretation that are expressed through rituals and stories.[15] He calls these frameworks "cultural-linguistic" systems that help people organize their spiritual experiences, allowing them to better understand themselves in the world. These systems each have an internal logic that helps people achieve a sense of self that's

14. Race, *Thinking About Religious Pluralism*, 46.

15. George Lindbeck, *The Nature of Doctrine: Religion and Theology in a Postliberal Age* (Westminster John Knox, 1984), 32.

authentically a part of the broader religious story. Different religions produce "fundamentally divergent depth experiences of what it is to be human."[16] For Lindbeck, concepts of salvation are inextricably tied to the narrative, or cultural-linguistic system, of the religion. Hick seems to adhere to Christianity as a cultural-linguistic system but then somehow gives himself a God's-eye view in order to claim that all religions envisage the same "Eternal One." For these reasons, I would venture that religious pluralism isn't a viable religious position.

The General Christian Narrative

At this point we should ask, What is the general Christian narrative, and what are the things that set Christianity's salvific claims apart from all other religions? Christians believe that throughout history God has spoken to people in various ways to reveal what is important to God. For instance, God spoke to Moses via the burning bush (Exod. 3), to Joseph through dreams (Gen. 37), and audibly to Samuel (1 Sam. 3). He also communicated through miraculous signs to Gideon (Judg. 6); through visions to Isaiah, Ezekiel, Peter, and Paul (Isa. 6; Ezek. 37; Acts 10; 16, respectively); through angelic messengers to Mary (Luke 1); and in many other ways to many other people as recorded in the Bible. In theology, these encounters are called **theophanies**, which are tangible manifestations of God to humans.

The writer of Hebrews tells us that God spoke ultimately in Jesus Christ:

> Long ago God spoke to our ancestors in many and various ways by the prophets, but in these last days he has spoken to us by a Son, whom he appointed heir of all things, through whom he also created the worlds. He is the reflection of God's glory and the exact imprint of God's very being, and he sustains all things by his powerful word. When he had made purification for sins, he sat down at the right hand of the Majesty on high. (1:1–3)

16. Lindbeck, *Nature of Doctrine*, 41.

This shows the finality of Christ's revelation compared to every other one that came prior—not just a simple theophany where God was made visible to people but rather an **incarnation**, where God was made flesh and entered creation through Jesus Christ. This doesn't mean God completely vacated heaven to become human. It wasn't a direct exchange. Rather, God is triune—concurrently three Persons in one essence. Karl Barth interprets the term "person" as a "mode of being,"[17] which means the **Trinity** can be defined as God being one in essence, yet there are three distinct ways of being God, concurrently and eternally. The Persons of God are paradoxically both separate and one. Their roles are intertwined even as they differ, and they share the same will through love and mutuality. So while God became incarnate in Jesus, the Spirit continues to move throughout the cosmos, and the Father still reigns sovereignly on the throne.

Now that God has been revealed fully in Jesus Christ, there's no going back! We can't retreat to relating to God through mere theophanies, and God made it so we don't have to. Christ died, rose again, ascended to heaven, and then poured out his Spirit, the Holy Spirit, on all flesh (Acts 2). The Holy Spirit is the Spirit of Christ! The Spirit is God in us, with us, and around us. Because the Spirit is Christ, in a trinitarian sense, the Spirit reveals Christ to us. We know Jesus, even two thousand years later, because we know the Spirit. We know Jesus's character and what he cares about because the Spirit reveals these things to us.

Prayer is not merely a therapeutic way to gather our thoughts or quell our anxieties. Prayer is a conversation with Jesus through the Spirit. Throughout this book, I highlight prayer because it's the most fundamental and essential spiritual practice—it's talking to God. When we discuss other spiritual practices like reading Scripture or worship, these, along with every other discipline, should be soaked in prayer. In fact, every spiritual practice should be a form of prayer,

17. Karl Barth, *Church Dogmatics*, vol. 1, part 2, ed. G. W. Bromiley and T. F. Torrance, trans. G. T. Thomson and Harold Knight (T&T Clark International, 2004), 163.

a means to connect with God and the only way we come to discern God's voice.

These massive theological claims above are what make Christianity unique. No other major religion perceives God as triune or believes that God became flesh to save humanity. No other faith claims that their redeemer is both 100 percent God and 100 percent human (theologians call this the hypostatic union), or that God's Spirit is a Person who resides within every believer. These theological claims have been formulated and repeated throughout Christian history to help us make sense of how God has revealed Godself to us. While these claims are mysterious, they're still knowable to the extent that we can *truly* know who God is by what God has revealed to us in Christ by the Spirit. But while knowing God through prayer is our primary way to know God, we can also come to know God through Scripture.

The Bible is the divinely inspired and authoritative account of God's revelation (2 Tim. 3:16). It offers us insights into the experiences, communities, traditions, and reasonings behind God's engagement with humanity and creation. Since we think of the Bible as a sacred witness of God's dealings with people, we view it as a solid foundation for all Christian belief and practice. We must state emphatically, however, that the Bible does not replace God. Nor is the Bible the *only* way God is revealed to us. Yet the Bible is *a* way God is revealed to us—and a particularly authoritative way at that. Theologian Stephen Binz states it well: "The Bible is a God-given way to experience the divine presence. Its inspired words not only offer us a treasury of images, stories, portraits of faith, prayers, and prophetic challenges, but they also bring us into an encounter with the living God. They are his words, personally addressed to us, and they have the power to convert our hearts and transform our lives."[18] The Bible should, therefore, be respected and revered. It should be respected as a living text that God has chosen to speak to us through. It should be revered as the inspired words of God that, by the power

18. Stephen Binz, *Conversing with God in Scripture: A Contemporary Approach to Lectio Divina* (The Word Among Us Press, 2008), 144.

of the Spirit, can form and transform us spiritually. Yet it should be revered and not worshiped. Our worship belongs to God alone. The Bible is a holy (set apart) record of God's interactions with humanity, but by the Spirit, we can connect directly with the God the Bible talks about. Jesus's sacrifice made it possible for us to be saved from our sin and, just as crucially, to be indwelt by the Spirit of God as God's temple (1 Cor. 6:19).

Let's pause for a moment and think about that statement. In the Old Testament, the Spirit resided in the tabernacle and later in the temple in two distinct ways. First, the Spirit enveloped and filled the temple, which is shown by God's glory (*shekinah*), a visible sign of God's presence (resembling a cloud) (1 Kings 8:10–11). Second, the ark of the covenant was situated in the holy of holies—the innermost section of the temple, partitioned off by a thick, red veil. The ark was viewed as God's footstool (1 Chron. 28:2), as the place where God's Spirit was manifested, particularly on the Day of Atonement (Lev. 16). Although the Spirit was with the people and in the temple, and even came on individuals (Judg. 6:34; 11:29; 1 Sam. 16:13), the Spirit did not permanently dwell within people in Old Testament times. The temple was a localized dwelling of God's presence, like a home.

In the New Testament, Jesus's death leads to the tearing of the temple veil: "Then Jesus cried again with a loud voice and breathed his last. At that moment the curtain of the temple was torn in two, from top to bottom. The earth shook, and the rocks were split" (Matt. 27:50–51). The tearing of the veil symbolizes that we now have direct access to God. God's presence is no longer confined to the temple but poured out on us. God resides in people, not a building. Paul says we are the temple of God *because* God's Spirit dwells in us (1 Cor. 3:16). As the church, *we* are God's dwelling place, a home in which God lives by the Spirit (Eph. 2:21–22).

Being the dwelling place of God carries personal and corporate implications for our identity as God's people and as sons and daughters of God, and for how we relate to each other. The **church** is made up of people who affirm the apostolic confession of Christ as Lord and are indwelled by the Spirit of God. We are a community that, after embracing the gospel and being filled with the Spirit, gathers in Christ's name to carry out his commands.

While many Christians like to focus on the cross and what Jesus did to save us from our sin, what we recounted above was what the cross effected—the *reason* for the cross and Christ's sacrifice. Jesus's ultimate goal was not only to save us from sin but to make a way for us to once again live and walk in the Spirit. There are two sides to Christ's sacrifice: On one side is Christ dying for our sin and defeating death on the cross. It is God showing us mercy, making it so we do not get what we deserve (eternal separation from God). On the flip side of Christ's sacrifice is what is made possible by Jesus. Jesus pours out his Spirit on us so we may be indwelt and empowered, filled and baptized, totally consumed and subsumed into life in the Spirit. It is God showing us grace, granting us what we don't deserve (eternal life with God). The triune God—the Father, Son, and Spirit—works as one to redeem us. Salvation is not just fire insurance but eternal, abundant living in God's kingdom as God's beloved children.

This beautiful story of love and redemption is the gospel. It is a story that starts and ends with God, and we, as God's children, are the ones God pursues. Religions around the world speak of higher powers and creators. They have rituals and paths for spiritual growth and maturity. They even do philanthropic works in their own communities. But only Christianity's God is the kind of God who would, like a good shepherd, leave the ninety-nine to find each one of us (Matt. 18:12–13). Only Christianity's God was so overcome by love so as to be made flesh, to live and walk among us, and to suffer the most excruciating[19] death to break the curses of sin and death we fell into. Only Christianity's God would do all of this to grant us life everlasting (John 3:16).

No one else died on the cross and rose again. Not a bodhisattva, not an avatar, not a prophet. No one but the Second Person of the

19. Notice the etymological root "crux" here. "Excruciating" literally means "as painful as crucifixion."

triune God made flesh. No one but Jesus of Nazareth. Philippians 2:9–11 (another of the earliest Christian texts) says,

> Therefore God exalted him even more highly
> and gave him the name
> that is above every other name,
> so that at the name given to Jesus
> every knee should bend,
> in heaven and on earth and under the earth,
> and every tongue should confess
> that Jesus Christ is Lord,
> to the glory of God the Father.

The name above all names is the name of Jesus Christ.

So let's revisit Hick's claim and ask, Does God have many names? Nah.

A Particular Jesus and His Universal Spirit

To talk about the particularity of Christ, three things are foundational in Scripture: (1) Yahweh is sovereign over all and requires covenantal exclusivity, (2) Jesus is Yahweh in the flesh, and (3) Jesus is the only way to salvation. Understanding these three claims leads us to see that the universal Spirit is at work in the world to draw us back to the particular God made flesh in Jesus Christ.

In the first two of the Ten Commandments, Yahweh explicitly rejects pluralism and syncretism, commanding that Yahweh alone be worshiped:

> I am the LORD your God, who brought you out of the land of Egypt, out of the house of slavery; you shall have no other gods before me.
>
> You shall not make for yourself an idol, whether in the form of anything that is in heaven above or that is on the earth beneath or that is in the water under the earth. You shall not bow down to them or serve them, for I the LORD your God am a jealous God, punishing

> children for the iniquity of parents to the third and the fourth generation of those who reject me but showing steadfast love to the thousandth generation of those who love me and keep my commandments. (Exod. 20:2–6)

God is called a jealous God (v. 5), which means Yahweh won't share the throne with anyone or anything. If Yahweh is the one true God, why should Yahweh share the throne with a false god? The idea of Yahweh being exclusive comes up often in the Old Testament, probably stated most clearly in Deuteronomy: "Acknowledge today and take to heart that the LORD is God in heaven above and on the earth beneath; there is no other" (Deut. 4:39). And the psalmist makes a clear distinction between Yahweh and idols:

> For great is the LORD and greatly to be praised;
> he is to be revered above all gods.
> For all the gods of the peoples are idols,
> but the LORD made the heavens. (Ps. 96:4–5)

As a whole, these verses lay the groundwork for biblical monotheism, covenantal exclusivity, and the rejection of idolatry and religious pluralism. Yahweh isn't some local or tribal deity. The Old Testament asserts that Yahweh is the one and only creator and ruler of everything.

The next crucial move the New Testament makes—the major move that differentiates Christianity from Judaism—is to claim that Jesus is the incarnation of Yahweh. The New Testament claims that Jesus isn't just a prophet or a moral teacher; he's Yahweh made flesh, the one true God revealed throughout the Old Testament. The writers of the New Testament consistently use titles, attributes, and Scriptures linked to Yahweh and apply them directly to Jesus.

The Gospel of John explicitly equates Jesus with the preexisting Word (*Logos*) through whom all things were made (John 1:1–3, 14). This passage starts the same way as Genesis 1, which ties the creative work of Yahweh to Jesus. One of my favorite passages in John is in chapter 8 when Jesus uses the divine name "I AM" (ἐγὼ εἰμί) to refer to himself. In this passage, Jesus is teaching in the temple and making big claims about himself, such as being the light of the world (v. 12) and the only one who has the power to judge (v. 16). The Pharisees get mad and question him, asking if he thinks he is greater than Abraham. Jesus responds with one of the greatest comebacks of all time: "Very truly, I tell you, before Abraham was, I am" (v. 58). By using God's divine name, Jesus claims to be equivalent with Yahweh. He also implies that he is the preexisting *Logos*, since "before Abraham was" (past tense), "I am" (present tense). What a boss!

I've already mentioned several ways Paul discusses the deity and particularity of Christ. But when Paul, in Philippians 2:9–11, says every knee shall bend and every tongue confess Jesus's lordship, he is directly quoting Isaiah 45:23: "To me [Yahweh] every knee shall bow, every tongue shall swear." Here, Yahweh is speaking, so when Paul applies this to Jesus, he's indirectly claiming that Jesus *is* Yahweh. Likewise, the writer of Hebrews quotes from Psalm 102:25–27 and applies the passage to Jesus, associating creation with Jesus: "In the beginning, Lord, you founded the earth, and the heavens are the work of your hands" (Heb. 1:10). And in Revelation, Jesus calls himself the Alpha and Omega (1:8), the first and the last (v. 17), which is another direct quote from Isaiah (44:6; 48:12). Once again, the New Testament writers apply divine and eternal designations to Jesus.

The final foundational biblical claim concerns the exclusivity of Christ. The New Testament has quite a few passages that highlight how Jesus stands out from all other religious leaders and traditions. For example, in John 14:6, Jesus states, "I am the way and the truth and the life. No one comes to the Father except through me." This is probably the clearest and most exclusive claim. Jesus doesn't just say he is *a* way but claims to be *the* way, which rules out other routes to God. In Acts 4:12, Peter similarly states that salvation is only found in Jesus: "There is salvation in no one else, for there is no other name under heaven given among mortals by which we must be saved."

Furthermore, 1 Timothy 2:5 says, "For there is one God; there is also one mediator between God and humankind, Christ Jesus, himself human." This verse underscores Christ's unique role as the sole mediator—a position that no other religious leader or prophet has. Last, Paul mentions that Jesus is "the image of the invisible God, the firstborn of all creation" (Col. 1:15) and that "in him all the fullness of God was pleased to dwell, and through him God was pleased to reconcile to himself all things, whether on earth or in heaven, by making peace through the blood of his cross" (vv. 19–20). Paul emphasizes Christ's supreme status not merely as a moral teacher but as the complete embodiment of God.

Throughout the New Testament, Jesus is portrayed as the incarnation of Yahweh, the only one through whom salvation comes. But while most Christians don't believe salvation is possible through other means apart from Christ, they do believe that salvation is *available* to everyone through Christ.[20] This is what leads us to another of Christianity's major claims: The Holy Spirit, the Spirit of Christ, is universally at work in the world to reveal the particular Christ to everyone who would call on his name. The Spirit is where exclusivity and universality meet, and, I would argue, it is the Spirit of Christ that leads us to the Father in the crowded space of competing narratives.

Beyond the Impasse

I remember sitting in a Zoom call with interreligious faith leaders and asking the host how much interreligious dialogue is possible when religions hold their own exclusive claims to truth and salvation. We can start the conversation, but surely we'll meet a fork in the road where we have to choose one religion over the other. What do we do then? The host couldn't answer my question but did say that an open and welcoming demeanor toward the religious other is crucial for any sort of meaningful dialogue. But I felt that more needed to be said. How can we move from meaningful dialogue to sharing the gospel? We do, after all, want everyone to come to know the love of Christ.

20. Here, I am assuming free will theism. Calvinists would argue that salvation is only available to the elect.

Amos Yong, one of Pentecostalism's most prolific theologians, has spent quite a bit of time engaging interreligious dialogue and mission. Yong puts plainly the tensions that exist when claiming the particularity of Christ and the universality of the Spirit: "The perennial problem for Christian theology of religions has been how the affirmation of divine presence in the universe of human religiousness can be compatible with the affirmation of salvation through the particular person of Jesus Christ."[21] Theologies of religion have tried to answer this issue by denying the Spirit's universality (something exclusivists might claim), by denying the particularity of Christ (something pluralists might claim), or by trying to find a median point between the two (something inclusivists might claim). Each of these frameworks addresses the issue of religious diversity in their own way.

Exclusivism argues that salvation can be attained only through an explicit faith in Jesus Christ and that Christianity is the only true religion.[22] It emphasizes that Christ is the one and only way to reconcile with God and that the Spirit's role is limited to guiding people toward Christ. Any spiritual experiences that seem to occur outside of Christianity are either viewed as preparation for the reception of the gospel or dismissed as demonic or misleading.

As discussed above, religious pluralism claims that no one religion holds exclusive rights to truth or salvation. It views all significant religions as equally legitimate answers to the divine, influenced by their cultural and historical backgrounds; Jesus is often regarded as one of many revelations instead of as the ultimate one. And it supports the complete universality and equality of the Spirit's influence across all religions. The Spirit isn't limited to Christ, and it's the same divine spirit that's fully active in other spiritual traditions.

A third option between exclusivism and pluralism is known as **inclusivism**, which states that salvation comes solely through Christ,

21. Amos Yong, *Discerning the Spirit(s): A Pentecostal-Charismatic Contribution to Christian Theology of Religions* (Sheffield Academic Press, 2000), 35.

22. Millard Erickson, *Introducing Christian Doctrine*, 3rd ed., ed. Arnold Hustad (Baker Academic, 2015), 322.

but Christ's salvific truth may be available to people of other faiths.[23] This view upholds the uniqueness and centrality of Christ in salvation while also highlighting that the benefits of the cross might extend beyond the visible expression of Christianity in the world. Inclusivists recognize the Spirit's presence in all cultures and religions, working to prepare hearts for Christ's redemption—even in places where Jesus's name has never been uttered or has been severely misrepresented. The Spirit's universal nature is genuine and can lead to salvation. Some inclusivists believe this can be done implicitly through nature or reason (Rom. 1:20), or explicitly as everyone is somehow given the opportunity to confess Jesus in this age or the age to come.

While Yong admits to holding a view closest to inclusivism,[24] he argues that the whole exclusivist-inclusivist-pluralist paradigm might have outlived its usefulness.[25] These distinctions might be a bit too rigid, since one could at the same time be "an exclusivist regarding the foundations of salvation, an inclusivist regarding the question of the unevangelized, and a pluralist regarding the fact of religious diversity."[26] But an even bigger problem for Yong is that the Christological language used in this paradigm assumes Christian terminology and concepts and imposes them onto other religions.[27] This means that even if we were to aim to promote interreligious dialogue, the imposition of Christian theological perspectives would hinder genuine interaction. What if we don't actually agree on the definition of salvation or the divine? If we assume only the Christian vantage point, we'll have trouble hearing the perspectives and questions of others.[28] The old paradigm creates an impasse in interreligious dialogue—either we discuss Jesus or we don't engage at all.

23. Erickson, *Introducing Christian Doctrine*, 322.

24. Amos Yong, *Beyond the Impasse: Toward a Pneumatological Theology of Religions* (Wipf & Stock, 2003), 27.

25. Yong, *Beyond the Impasse*, 28.

26. Yong, *Beyond the Impasse*, 28.

27. Yong, *Beyond the Impasse*, 29.

28. A more difficult question is whether learning about others on Christian terms is really learning from others or only presuming that what one already knows is also known by others.

To move past repetitive and polarizing conversations that occur in the exclusivist-inclusivist-pluralist paradigm, Yong suggests we adopt a Spirit-centered approach to a theology of religions. A pneumatological framework supports three fundamental principles: (1) God is always present and working through the Spirit, (2) God's Spirit is the "life-breath" of the *imago Dei* in every person and the foundation of all human relationships and communities, and (3) everything in existence is providentially upheld by the Spirit of God for divine purposes.[29] While not ever rejecting the particularity of Christ, Yong's framework first taps into what the Spirit is doing in the world. Since God is triune, the work of the Spirit is always united with the will of Christ and the Father. As Yong writes, "All human endeavors reflect either God's permissive or active will toward ultimately divine purposes centered around the full revelation of Jesus Christ and the impending kingdom of God."[30] By beginning with the Spirit, we can move past the Christological impasse and still affirm both the universality of the Spirit and the particularity of Christ in a broader trinitarian context.[31]

Yong's approach is key to recognizing God's voice in our global pluralistic world. We can learn to hear God's voice through interactions with different cultures and religions instead of thinking every non-Christian is spiritually empty. To be clear, we're not listening for *other* spirits from other religions or traditions but to the Holy Spirit that's at work in every part of the world. This view can help Christians discern God's voice echoing through various cultural expressions like art, traditions, moral frameworks, and rituals worldwide.

The "Many Tongues" Thesis

When we start with the Spirit for cross-cultural dialogues, we come to realize that the Spirit is a translator, not just a converter. While every religious tradition has their own cultural-linguistic system and

29. Yong, *Beyond the Impasse*, 45–46.
30. Yong, *Beyond the Impasse*, 46.
31. Yong, *Discerning the Spirit(s)*, 58.

corresponding terminology, the universal Spirit can break through those linguistic parameters and help us to see and understand each other. Discernment between the spirits is about listening to the Spirit across boundaries with ears attuned to Christ's voice.

Christian mission should not be about erasing differences but about embracing them in the Spirit as we center around Christ. This reflects Acts 2, where, through the Spirit's power, folks from many nations heard God's message in their own languages (vv. 6–11). Instead of diminishing cultural differences, Pentecost amplified diversity by affirming the many tongues being spoken. Considering this, Yong developed his "many tongues" thesis that views the languages at Pentecost as a symbol for how the Spirit interacts with cultures, people groups, and even religionists.[32] Instead of pushing for uniformity, the Spirit celebrates plurality.

Likewise, the Spirit empowers Christians not only to speak but also to listen across differences, recognizing God's voice even in unexpected places. It's important to note that Yong never says God has many names; instead, he says people speak many tongues. Our triune God is one even as the world is pluralistic. The Spirit meets us where we're at—all of us. As we acknowledge the Spirit's constant work everywhere, we begin to engage in a two-way dialogue through which both Christians and others are transformed by the Spirit.

What might this look like in practice? Once again, the book of Acts is instructive. Throughout Acts, Paul faces challenges and opportunities that concern intercultural, interethnic, and intertribal issues. So what actions does Paul take when he faces ethnic and religious differences? Yong, during a public lecture he gave at my university, described three "windows" into Paul's missional encounters with other religions found in the book of Acts.[33]

32. Amos Yong, *In the Days of Caesar: Pentecostalism and Political Theology* (Eerdmans, 2010), 110.

33. The three windows paradigm was drawn from a lecture Yong delivered at Life Pacific University in 2023 as part of a grant from Interfaith America. See "Module 3: Building Interfaith Bridges, Deepening Pentecostal Faith," Life Pacific University, accessed May 30, 2025, https://lifepacific.edu/reconciliation-certificate/.

The first window, which is perhaps the most famous of Paul's interreligious dialogues, is called the "Athens Window" (Acts 17). Luke highlights how Paul uses a dialogical approach, both arguing and conversing with the Athenians at the Areopagus (v. 17).[34] He addresses the Athenians using their own teachings as a reference point and even approvingly quotes from their pagan sources (v. 28). Paul finds an inroad for dialogue when he notices an altar that reads "To an unknown God" (v. 23). He shares the message of Christ with them, and by honoring their beliefs and teachings, Paul acknowledges them within a shared human reality. He emphasizes that God is not distant but close to them. God is available for them to discover right in their midst. The Athens Window shows us today that all people are part of the same humanity and that God is nearby, yearning for a relationship with all of us.

The second window is called the "Ephesus Window" (Acts 19) and showcases how Paul and his missionary friends interact with gentiles in Ephesus. They share the message of Christ every day in the lecture hall of Tyrannus (v. 9). Since this continues for two years, it leads to some political fallout. The followers of Artemis accuse Paul and his friends of harming Ephesus's economy. Crowds form to attack them, but the town clerk steps in to defend the apostles, stating that they haven't done anything wrong. Significantly, it's an Ephesian who acknowledges that the disciples haven't blasphemed Artemis. It shows that Paul didn't come to Ephesus with the intention of preaching against their gods but rather to promote Christ.

Yong says this window teaches us that the best witness is not brashly tearing down other religious beliefs but compellingly sharing "a positive witness to the transformative power of the gospel." Our goal should be "not to exacerbate interreligious enmities but to be sufficiently deferential in order to establish dialogical relationships with those in other faiths."[35] We don't want to burn bridges with folks from other faith traditions; instead, we want to create pathways for

34. Amos Yong, *The Missiological Spirit: Christian Mission Theology in the Third Millennium Global Context* (Cascade Books, 2014), 129.
35. Yong, *Missiological Spirit*, 129.

friendship and dialogue. Wouldn't it be powerful if your religious opponents liked you so much that they defended you against slander and falsities? In Ephesus, it is Paul's faithful witness of Christ and respect for others that ultimately clears his name.

Finally, Yong calls window three the "Malta Window" (Acts 28), based on the story of when Paul and his crew find refuge on the island of Malta after a shipwreck. Luke says the locals show them "unusual kindness" (v. 2). A snake bites Paul, but he doesn't suffer any harm, leading some of the Maltesians to start treating him like a god. Paul then heals Publius, the island's chief, along with a few others. So when it is time for Paul and his group to leave, the Maltesians honor the crew in various ways and load their ship with supplies. This scene demonstrates, according to Yong, that bearing witness through the power of the Spirit requires taking on a posture of hospitality that not only welcomes strangers but also receives hospitality from strangers. In this way, "our testimony is borne not only in what we say but also, perhaps more importantly, in how we live, how we interact with others, and how we are able to receive of the gifts of others as well."[36]

The Maltesians' warm hospitality makes us wonder who's really being saved here. To be clear, Jesus is the only one who can save anyone. But what's cool to recognize is that it isn't just the Maltesians who are blessed by Paul and the missionaries through healing acts—the apostles are also blessed by the kindness and generosity of the locals. Yong says, "Here is the interreligious encounter I continue to pray for—that when I meet people of other faiths, God will keep saving me."[37] It's not that any other God can save Yong but that Jesus would continue to save him as the Spirit reveals Christ, even through interactions with the religious other. Christ's particularity is not diminished—he is the incarnated God through whom our salvation is possible. But in these encounters, we see the religious other

36. Amos Yong, *Who Is the Holy Spirit? A Walk with the Apostles* (Paraclete, 2011), 186.

37. Steven Félix-Jäger, "Exploring a Pentecostal Commitment to Interfaith Dialogue," Interfaith America, December 11, 2023, https://www.interfaithamerica.org/article/pentecostal-commitment-interfaith/.

being loved and dignified, pursued and called by the Spirit. The Spirit is already at work in those spaces, always present and always speaking. Yong is calling us to tap into what the Spirit is already doing not just in others through our witness but also in us through the many forms of receiving witness.

Spiritual Reading

So far, this chapter has discussed what makes Christianity unique, why the particularity of Christ is crucial for our faith, and how the universal Spirit bears witness to Christ all over the world. The last question we'll ask and seek to answer is, How can we make this story unique and particular *to us*? What can we do to make the Christian narrative not just another narrative in a global marketplace of beliefs, stories, and symbols? In other words, can we internalize the Christian story and let it sink into our bones until we don't just recount the tale of Christ's death and resurrection but embody it? The goal of Christian discipleship is to be formed in the Spirit and to live out Christ's story as his followers. We want to do the things the Spirit leads us to do, care about the things Christ cares about, and reject the things that grieve God's heart. We want to internalize God's story in a pluralist world—not to hide away in certainty but to let it shape us so deeply that when we return to the plurality, the truth of our witness resonates deeply with all who hear.

One powerful way we can internalize Christ's story is by reading Scripture in a way that's soaked in prayer. We'll start to hear God's voice vividly when we read the Bible with our whole selves attuned to what God is saying to us. A **spiritual reading** of the Bible is an approach to Scripture reading that focuses on being formed by the Spirit through the text. Spiritual reading engages Scripture devotionally to aid in our overall spiritual development. It is formative and can be viewed as a journey of spiritual growth, which is different from a reading style that focuses on the transmission of information.

Pastor and biblical scholar Eugene Peterson, who crafted the Bible paraphrase *The Message*, wrote a well-known book about the spiritual practice of Scripture reading called *Eat This Book*. In it, Peterson makes a peculiar passage from Revelation his central theme. In Revelation 10:8–11, a voice from heaven (likely God) instructs John to eat a scroll that an angel has offered to him:

> Then the voice that I had heard from heaven spoke to me again, saying, "Go, take the scroll that is open in the hand of the angel who is standing on the sea and on the land." So I went to the angel and told him to give me the little scroll, and he said to me, "Take it and eat; it will be bitter to your stomach but sweet as honey in your mouth." So I took the little scroll from the hand of the angel and ate it; it was sweet as honey in my mouth, but when I had eaten it my stomach was made bitter. Then they said to me, "You must prophesy again about many peoples and nations and languages and kings."

"Eating the scroll" can be seen as internalizing, literally consuming, God's message—it's nice to receive, but the prophetic duty that comes next can be tough (bitter). Peterson picks up on this image and says that we, as disciples of Christ, should eat the Bible. We should internalize it, consume it, and assimilate it into every aspect of our lives, because "readers become what they read."[38]

Although exegeting Scripture to understand the meaning of the text in its original context is important, eating the Bible requires more than an informative reading of the text. A spiritual reading of the Bible requires submission to the text. Not only do we read the words in Scripture, but we submit to what those words are saying to us. We allow those words to *read us*. Only then can Scripture look into our lives, convict and transform us. We're not just observing the text but receiving what it reveals about us. This seems to be what the writer of Hebrews had in mind when he said, "Indeed, the word of God is living and active and sharper than any two-edged sword, piercing

38. Eugene Peterson, *Eat This Book: A Conversation in the Art of Spiritual Reading* (Eerdmans, 2006), 20.

until it divides soul from spirit, joints from marrow; it is able to judge the thoughts and intentions of the heart" (4:12). If we let the Bible read us, we allow our desires to be examined and our motives to be scrutinized. We recognize that through the Bible the personally revealing God directly addresses us in "whatever circumstances we find ourselves, at whatever age we are, in whatever state we are."[39] In Scripture we encounter God, and God communes with us.

An ancient and popular way to absorb and internalize Scripture is through lectio divina, which means, roughly, "sacred reading."[40] **Lectio divina** is an age-old Christian practice of spiritual reading and reflection on Scripture that helps deepen one's relationship with God. The general principles of lectio divina began to be recorded by the patristic authors of the early Christian centuries[41] but have evolved over the years into a dedicated way of reading the Bible that helps us grasp and absorb the text in a way that shapes our lives, rather than just leaving a mark on our thoughts or emotions.[42] The starting point of lectio divina, and something we should do before any sacred reading of a text, is to invoke the Spirit in prayer. The Spirit is, after all, the one who enables us to experience the Bible as God's living word. The Spirit gives us fresh ways to perceive God's truth through the text and also enables us to interpret Scripture in a way that's personal to us.[43] The Spirit doesn't replace the need for exegesis and understanding the text in context but reveals the heart of Christ in the pages of Scripture.[44]

There are four moves in lectio divina that help us prayerfully read the Bible in God's presence. It should be stated at the outset that these four moves should not be followed legalistically or rigidly like a methodical system. Theologian Stephen Binz reminds us that "there are no obligatory steps, and the most fruitful exercise of lectio does not

39. Peterson, *Eat This Book*, 28.
40. Binz, *Conversing with God in Scripture*, 11.
41. Binz, *Conversing with God in Scripture*, 15.
42. Peterson, *Eat This Book*, 81.
43. Binz, *Conversing with God in Scripture*, 22.
44. Binz, *Conversing with God in Scripture*, 32.

necessarily follow a required sequence or seek any specific goal. The most important thing to keep in mind when practicing lectio divina is that it is meant to lead us to a personal encounter and dialogue with God."[45] With that being said, the four moves of lectio divina are *lectio*, which means reading; *meditatio*, which means meditation; *oratio*, which means prayer; and *contemplatio*, which means contemplation. These four moves are meant to be interrelated, blending together or occurring simultaneously.[46] The main thing to grasp is that when we read Scripture spiritually, we also pray, meditate on, and contemplate the words that we read. This allows the words to linger in our thoughts and to talk back to our fears and doubts. With lectio divina, Scripture is not read quickly but slowly and deeply. The words of Scripture circle and surround us before sinking into our pores.

A spiritual reading of Scripture formatively establishes a narrative base for our discernment. Whenever it's time to make a decision, the words that rise from our depths will be the words of Scripture. One concern with spiritual reading, however, may be the fear of misinterpreting the Bible; since spiritual reading can be subjective, what if we end up interpreting a text in a way that harms us spiritually? We've all seen folks approach Scripture with a specific agenda, twisting or cherry-picking verses to justify their actions. So how do we keep our spiritual readings theologically grounded if we don't have advanced training in biblical studies?

First, a simple way to enhance our understanding is to pick up a good study Bible. Study Bibles come with introductions, notes, and summaries that provide context for the passages. They highlight the date, author, and original audience; discuss the cultural and historical context of the text; and frame the main themes of the passage. Often, they feature maps and timelines, giving us a clearer picture of how history played out or where events took place geographically. Plus, they often include cross-references, showing how different passages connect throughout the Bible. This is helpful because it allows

45. Binz, *Conversing with God in Scripture*, 43.
46. Binz, *Conversing with God in Scripture*, 45.

us to spot, for example, if a New Testament writer is quoting from an Old Testament book, trying to establish patterns or typologies, or trying to illustrate how an Old Testament prophecy was fulfilled in the New Testament. While study Bibles are generally affordable, there are many Bible translations that have free apps online with study features.

Second, reading Scripture in community is important because it grounds our individual interpretations into shared discernment. When we're offtrack, fellow believers can help us clarify our meanings or challenge our biases. They can share wisdom with us by bringing their own unique insights to the table. After all, Proverbs 27:17 tells us that "iron sharpens iron." In a community of shared discernment, we understand that the Spirit is communicating not just to us but also to others in the body of Christ (1 Cor. 14:26). Reading together is another way to hear God's voice through the text.

Finally, we can trust that when we read Scripture faithfully and prayerfully, the Spirit will guide us to understand everything in Scripture that's crucial for our faith. This reflects a Protestant doctrine known as the clarity or **perspicuity of Scripture**, meaning the Bible is clear and understandable in its essential teachings. The Westminster Confession of Faith, an influential seventeenth-century Reformed confession, states it like this: "All things in Scripture are not alike plain in themselves, nor alike clear unto all; yet those things which are necessary to be known, believed, and observed for salvation, are so clearly propounded, and opened in some place of Scripture or other, that not only the learned, but the unlearned, in a due use of the ordinary means, may attain unto a sufficient understanding of them."[47] The ordinary means that the confession refers to include the use of a Bible translation in one's own language, listening to teachers, reading commentaries and other Bible tools, awareness of the wisdom contained in the church's history of interpretation, and seeking communal

47. "The Westminster Confession of Faith," Ligonier, accessed June 7, 2025, https://learn.ligonier.org/articles/westminster-confession-faith.

understanding in fellowship.[48] With just a little effort, we can come to a legitimate understanding of the general narrative of Scripture. Perspicuity can be summed up with the popular Protestant phrase "The main things are the plain things, and the plain things are the main things." God intends Scripture to communicate truth clearly to those who genuinely seek it, by the guidance of the Holy Spirit. While recognizing the lenses through which we read Scripture, we can trust that the Spirit transcends whatever perspectives we're bound by. In this day of global pluralism, let's confidently engage in spiritual reading to internalize God's story. Let's eat the book!

Conclusion

At the beginning of this chapter, I shared a story about newborn Mila recognizing my voice. The reason she recognized my voice is because it was familiar and formative. She's always heard my voice! There were many brand-new sounds she was experiencing for the first time, yet somehow all the other voices and sounds—shouting for her attention, tugging and pulling—lost their hold. She didn't physically stop hearing them, but she chose to stop *listening* to them when she zeroed in on my voice.

In the same way, once we've internalized God's story through spiritual reading, when God speaks it won't sound like a riddle but like a conversation that resonates deeply with what we've already read and contemplated in Scripture. Our hearts will recognize God's voice because they'll have been shaped by God's story, formed by listening to the Spirit, and trained by the love of Christ found in the pages of Scripture. This is also how we can witness the Spirit's work all over the world. The Spirit is everywhere, speaking to everyone and pointing to Christ (John 16:13–14). When anyone anywhere is being led toward a clearer sense of God's loving-kindness and a

48. Wayne Grudem, "The Perspicuity of Scripture," *Themelios* 34, no. 3, accessed June 7, 2025, https://www.thegospelcoalition.org/themelios/article/the-perspicuity-of-scripture/.

stronger desire to know Jesus, we're witnessing the Spirit's work in the world.

The Spirit goes before us, stirring our longings even before we consciously come to know Christ.[49] As Augustine famously said, "You have made us for yourself, O Lord, and our heart is restless until it rests in you."[50] When someone feels spiritually restless, it's quite possible that they are being gently pulled by the Spirit.

Some things in life will always feel mysterious or incomplete. But when the Spirit guides us to Christ, we can find a sense of security even through the unknown (this is something we'll discuss further in chap. 5). This chapter considered what it means to hear God in the crowded space of legitimate competing narratives. But what about when those narratives are illegitimate and fraught with misinformation? That's what we'll dive into in the next chapter.

KEY WORDS

- **church**: A group of people who affirm the apostolic confession of Christ as Lord and are indwelled by the triune God
- **exclusivism**: The belief that salvation can be attained only through an explicit faith in Jesus Christ and that Christianity is the only true religion
- **incarnation**: The theological doctrine that claims God was made flesh and entered creation through Jesus Christ
- **inclusivism**: The belief that salvation comes solely through Christ but that Christ's salvific truth may also be available to people of other faiths
- **lectio divina**: An ancient Christian practice of spiritual reading and reflection on Scripture that helps deepen one's relationship with God

49. In Wesleyan theology, this is called prevenient grace.
50. Augustine, *Confessions* (Oxford University Press, 2009), 4.

- **perspicuity of Scripture**: The Protestant doctrine that holds that the Bible is clear and understandable in its essential teachings
- **religious pluralism**: The idea that all religions reflect the same ultimate reality, but different religious traditions receive and experience this universal presence through their own cultural lenses
- **salvation**: Being delivered from sin and death through Jesus's sacrifice and receiving everlasting life in a restored relationship with God
- **spiritual reading**: An approach to reading Scripture that focuses on being formed by the Spirit through the text
- **theophany**: A tangible manifestation of God to humans
- **Trinity**: The theological doctrine that claims God is one in essence, but there are three ways of being God, concurrently and eternally

DISCUSSION QUESTIONS

- Has anyone ever challenged you about the exclusivity of Christ? How did you respond?
- Have you ever recognized Jesus's voice in places you weren't expecting to hear it? How could you tell it was the Holy Spirit revealing Christ?
- What is something God has revealed to you through a spiritual reading of Scripture?

REFLECTION EXERCISE

Practice lectio divina with John 10:1–5. Slowly read the passage and meditate on what it means to recognize Jesus's voice. Ask God to make you more sensitive to God's voice and journal any impressions.

three

Hearing God Through the Noise of Misinformation

The first time a student tried to fact-check me was in 2015 during my Introduction to Philosophy class. I was midway through a lecture on epistemology when a student questioned me about a basic idea I've covered countless times. He asked, "Is that true?" and when I replied that it was, he pulled out his iPhone 6 and Googled it. I was taken aback—I wasn't used to being doubted like that, especially not on the basics. Not in the middle of a sentence. And especially not by a kid who trusted a top search result more than an expert who had spent years reading, writing, and nerding out on the topic. After about thirty seconds, he looked up and declared triumphantly to his classmates, "He's right!" Should I have felt vindicated by Google or validated after initially being distrusted? I was perplexed at what had nonchalantly happened right in front of me.

Before I got back to my lecture, I took a moment to pause. This felt like more than a challenge. It felt like a small cultural shift was unfolding right there between the two of us. Authority wasn't assumed anymore. Expertise wasn't trusted. It all had to be *verified*—instantly, on an iPhone screen. The post-truth era, the war on expertise, and the algorithm replacing the library had all seeped in. Looking back, that moment feels symbolic.

When the news is slanted and social media echoes back our own views, it's hard to tell what's actually true and what's not. It gets even more difficult when we realize that many advertisers, political regimes, and even foreign powers intentionally mislead us, securing their own interests by swaying our actions. Throughout this book, I've argued that we are in a pluralistic age that sits on a bedrock of secularity (Secularity 3) but tolerates all sorts of worldviews—religious and nonreligious alike. That pluralism also contains worldviews that are borne out of falsehoods, misinformation, and conspiracy theories. This chapter thus considers what it means to hear God through the bewildering noise of misinformation. After we define our post-truth era, we'll examine how misinformation, disinformation, and the "kitschification" of truth contribute to it. Finally, we'll redefine truth as *faithfulness*, which involves actively listening to the Spirit in prayer and consistently reading Scripture.

A Post-Truth Era

In a post-truth era, facts tend to slip away. Things that looked clear before seem hazy and uncertain. Yesterday's truths are today's conspiracy theories; today's lies are tomorrow's headlines. History reconfigures in real time. But what does "post-truth" actually mean? Does it mean everyone today lies or that truth isn't valued anymore? Philosopher John Dudiak argues that being in a post-truth era "does not mean that no one believes in truth anymore, but that there are no longer any authorities who are capable of providing us with truth claims that are acknowledged to be true by a broad general consensus, truths upon which we all basically agree."[1] Living in a post-truth era isn't so much about rejecting truth outright as it is about getting

1. Jeffrey Dudiak, *Post-Truth? Facts and Faithfulness* (Wipf & Stock, 2022), 3.

mixed up over who has the authority to narrate the truth. Can we trust anyone other than ourselves? Can we even trust ourselves?

Although this definition may be contested, in the modern West, we've generally seen **truth** as that which is in line with what's real or factual. Truth consists of statements of fact, like "Water boils at 212 degrees Fahrenheit." This statement is true because it is empirically verifiable. This sort of understanding of truth lines up with the **correspondence theory of truth**, which states that truth is in accord with reality or facts. The **post-truth era** questions our ability to know truth or to trust what someone claims to be true; we might refer to our era as a cultural environment where facts hold less power in influencing public opinion than emotional appeals or personal convictions. In such an era, truth is flexible—it's more about what feels right or fits a narrative than what's factually real.

There are many ways a person might distrust a general consensus of truth today. A person could be a cynic who is suspicious of those who claim to provide truth, a skeptic who is suspicious of our human capacity to know truth objectively, or a relativist who is suspicious that objective truth even exists.[2] We're all navigating this post-truth world, which means cynics, skeptics, and relativists are everywhere in our public discourse. We might even find ourselves embracing these attitudes from time to time. Instead of accepting someone else's claims to truth, we often rely on our own gut feelings, emotions, or personal preferences to determine what's right. How did we get here? Why do we have such a lack of faith in the media and those in charge? To answer these questions, we'll explore the origins of media distrust and how political powers manipulate the truth to influence opinions and shape attitudes.

Questioning Media Outlets

Not too long ago, there were a handful of trusted big news outlets on TV like CBS, NBC, and ABC; newspapers such as *The New York Times*, *The Los Angeles Times*, and *The Wall Street Journal*; and

2. Dudiak, *Post-Truth?*, 5.

international channels like the BBC. These outlets were like lighthouses that stood tall and shone their beams of information across the dark oceans of uncertainty. Most folks relied on just a few of these reliable, centralized outlets for news, so there weren't a thousand versions of the same story. Generally speaking, the news was trusted.

It was during this time that the impeccably mustachioed news broadcaster Walter Cronkite became known as the "most trusted man in America." In a 1972 "thermometer reading" poll about Americans' trust in public figures,[3] prominent pollster Oliver Quayle found that Walter Cronkite outperformed all political figures, religious leaders, and celebrities. The results led CBS, one of the three biggest networks ruling American television at the time,[4] to brand its star broadcaster the "most trusted man in America"—a moniker that stuck to him for the rest of his career. Cronkite's demeanor was calm, straightforward, and sincere. As an anchor for *CBS Evening News*, Cronkite didn't sensationalize the news; he just told the facts straight, ending each broadcast with his signature closing line, "And that's the way it was." He covered monumental moments in US history, including JFK's assassination, the Vietnam War, the moon landing in 1969, and the Watergate scandal. He was a well-informed, sincere, and calm presence during the tumultuous 1960s and all the way through the 1970s and early 1980s.

While more networks formed throughout the 1980s and 1990s, Americans still tended to trust their news anchors all throughout the twentieth century. In fact, in 2003, when Pew Research Center took a similar thermometer reading poll to Quayle's, popular evening news anchors Dan Rather (CBS), Peter Jennings (ABC), and Tom Brokaw (NBC) all scored high, leading every governmental and political leader except Colin Powell.[5] So what has happened since 2003 to make news broadcasters today so partisan and publicly distrusted?

3. Bootie Cosgrove-Mather, "The Most Trusted Man in America," CBS News, February 4, 2003, https://www.cbsnews.com/news/the-most-trusted-man-in-america/.

4. "Big Three TV Networks," Scholarly Community Encyclopedia, updated October 8, 2022, https://encyclopedia.pub/entry/28420.

5. Cosgrove-Mather, "Most Trusted Man in America."

Something significant happened during the TV news expansion of the 1980s and 1990s that still impacts us today. CNN (Cable News Network) was then the pioneer of twenty-four-hour news programming, a groundbreaking concept at the time. Suddenly, people could get news updates all day long, not just during the evening shows. To keep up with the unending news cycle, CNN brought in subject-area experts, or **news pundits**, to give opinions about current events and other hot topics. This approach to the news took off, and by 1983, CNN was the first TV news channel to turn a profit.[6] Seeing how successful and lucrative this model was, both Fox News and MSNBC launched twenty-four-hour news stations in 1996—leading to a new focus on speed and sensationalism in news reporting.[7] The more exciting the news coverage, the better the ratings!

In the early 1990s, some conservative talk radio show hosts were already calling out CNN and other media outlets for pushing liberal agendas.[8] So when Fox and MSNBC entered the scene, they intentionally positioned themselves as partisan options in the news world—Fox would skew right and MSNBC would skew left. While CNN may have inadvertently promoted left-leaning biases, what came next was a shift toward full-blown partisan news coverage, with the addition of particularized voices to the previously centralized news narrative.

But that's only the story of the news in the 1990s and early aughts. As we've moved into the twenty-first century, things have taken a turn. Major news outlets were already splitting along political lines, and then the internet took off! Because big news organizations often promote their own biases and sometimes put out poorly vetted information, trust in these establishments quickly began to erode. Then when social media came onto the scene, suddenly everyone became their own pundit, sharing their opinions on current events. Both reliable and unreliable sources began posting "news" at lightning speed. Rather than prioritizing accuracy and depth, the news became even more about sensationalism than before. Today, the lighthouse beams

6. Lee McIntyre, *Post-Truth* (MIT Press, 2018), 67.
7. McIntyre, *Post-Truth*, 69.
8. McIntyre, *Post-Truth*, 68.

are still shining but are hidden and obscured among millions of other flashing signals in many different directions. Now it's up to us to decide who to trust, and unfortunately, we're often drawn to the flashiest lights instead of the steady ones.

We all know social media is unreliable as a news source, yet we still go there for the news. A recent report from Pew Research shows that 54 percent of American adults get at least some of their news from social media. Among them, more than two-thirds rely on Facebook or YouTube, while others turn to Instagram (20 percent), TikTok (17 percent), and X (12 percent) for news.[9] This trend is particularly pronounced for younger adults; TikTok (Gen Z's favorite platform) has jumped from just 3 percent in 2020 to 17 percent in 2024 as a source for news. Maybe we're turning to social media because we distrust traditional outlets that can look more like propaganda machines than sources of actual news coverage. Can you blame anyone for looking elsewhere for news? But social media hasn't solved our issues; ironically, its algorithms have intensified partisanship and fueled **confirmation bias**—when people look for, interpret, and recall information that corroborates their existing beliefs.

When we don't trust authorities to help us understand what's going on in the world, we look to ourselves for answers. One way this happens is when algorithms parrot our own already held beliefs back to us. **Social media algorithms** are the rules that determine what we see when we log into social media apps like Instagram, TikTok, YouTube, or X. Since there's too much content available for any one person to consume, algorithms choose for us what they think we'll find most interesting or relevant. They keep tabs on our activities—what we like, share, watch, and comment on, and how long we linger on a post. They even notice what we scroll past in a hurry. Using that information, they guess what we might enjoy next. Algorithms score all the posts we might see and line them up from most to least likely to grab our attention. The top posts make it to

9. "Social Media and News Fact Sheet," Pew Research Center, September 25, 2025, https://www.pewresearch.org/journalism/fact-sheet/social-media-and-news-fact-sheet.

our feeds. Occasionally, they'll throw in something fresh or random to see if our tastes are shifting. During political seasons, we often see a ton of sensationalized content from the opposite political side because we tend to interact with those posts, even if it's out of frustration. In this way, algorithms help to strengthen our preexisting ideologies. Algorithms are always trying to keep us hooked, since our time translates to ad revenue.[10]

Philosopher Thorsten Botz-Bornstein argues that social media, through algorithms, enables our own narcissism, making *us* our only anchors to truth. Algorithms shape so much of our lives that they create whole new realities for us.[11] They decide which products we should like, which friends we should interact with, and which ideas should captivate us. But they base their suggestions on their perception of us, which means they're really just feeding into our self-obsession. As we doomscroll, we spend hours gazing into a mirror, scrutinizing every angle of our own features. When our eyes are fixed on ourselves, we don't notice the people around us. We can't see the world through their lenses. Social media is narcissistic because it enables us to keep spiraling around our own "selves" without being confronted by the "other."[12] We forget how to empathize.

So when we get our news from social media, what problems have we solved? Traditional news media showed us a single, vetted perspective on what was going on in the world. Surely it missed things and reinforced the ideas of the powerful, but at least our world felt secure. We were on the same page—unless, of course, we were those who were marginalized by dominant ideologies, a critique we should not miss. Lack of access can push aside legitimate expert voices that those in power have chosen to ignore.

10. Clodagh O'Brien, "How Do Social Media Algorithms Work?," Digital Marketing Institute, April 28, 2023, https://digitalmarketinginstitute.com/blog/how-do-social-media-algorithms-work.

11. Thorsten Botz-Bornstein, *The New Aesthetics of Deculturation: Neoliberalism, Fundamentalism and Kitsch* (Bloomsbury Academic, 2019), 18.

12. Botz-Bornstein, *New Aesthetics of Deculturation*, 12.

Partisan news media has sought to solve the problem of access by showing us multiple sides to stories, but we must question the value of such an approach. Does it help or hurt to have two opposing pundits on the same panel, where one is a scientist with expertise on the subject and the other is a popular author and conspiracy theorist? What value does the second pundit actually provide? And because partisan news media tends toward sensationalism for ratings, it can make us even more anxious about the world we live in. It sows and cultivates the seeds of discord as ideological groups are pitted against each other.

The decentralized space of social media makes the news easily accessible but nearly impossible to vet. Social media algorithms make it so the news isn't actually democratized but whittled down once again to a single narrative. This time, however, the single narrative is our own underinformed sense of the world reflected back to us. The partisan fighting subsists, but even as "news" content multiplies exponentially, we know even less about what's truly happening.

Questioning the Experts

Our post-truth era has also made us question and radically reinterpret the role of expertise in the world. Experts used to be our society's gatekeepers of truth and knowledge, but the internet has opened up access to information for everyone. While easier access to knowledge is a good thing, it also means, as discussed above, that people can get stuck in echo chambers and only see what they want to see. Folks often skip over expert opinions and make up their minds based on YouTube videos, Reddit discussions, or influencers, usually without the critical skills to evaluate the sources. It can be difficult to determine who online is actually an expert and who is pulling things out of thin air. After all, YouTube videos and podcasts of both experts and nonexperts often look the same.

A great following doesn't determine expertise. I've got some smart friends who are amazing scholars but who struggle with social media and only have a handful of followers, even though their content is top-notch. Conversely, there are plenty of charlatans and conspiracy theorists with massive followings—not because their claims are valid but because they're entertaining and have magnetic personalities. It's tough to know who to trust and what information qualifies as legitimate. When someone claims they've done their own research, it might just mean they've binge-watched conspiracy videos on YouTube.

Moreover, when we gain some expert knowledge on a subject, we can tend to become overconfident with what we know. A. J. Swoboda points out that today's overabundance of information has made it difficult for us to differentiate between experts and people who have merely gained access to expert knowledge.[13] An expert is "someone who through hard work, study, and perseverance has earned a weight of authority in a particular domain of knowledge or activity."[14] Expertise takes years to develop. When someone is an expert in their field, they're not just familiar with the key debates and figures in their area; they've also contributed their own original ideas. In fact, to earn a PhD, you have to produce new knowledge—something that hasn't yet been discovered, shown, or understood like that before in the field. My doctoral dissertation, for example, did this by combining Pentecostal theology with theological aesthetics to form a new concept of "Pentecostal aesthetics."

The issue is that when a person learns some expert knowledge, they might assume they've become an expert. This person might not have watched conspiratorial YouTube videos but legitimate ones by real scholars. But they're still not experts until they have a comprehensive understanding of the entire field. Swoboda argues that we should therefore approach expertise with humility. We must recognize that not everyone is an expert, and even if they are an expert in one thing, that doesn't mean they're an expert in everything.[15] When we trust experts, we're not saying they can't be wrong or that we must uncritically accept whatever they say. Instead, we're acknowledging

13. A. J. Swoboda, *A Teachable Spirit: The Virtue of Learning from Strangers, Enemies, and Absolutely Anyone* (Zondervan Reflective, 2025), 35.

14. Swoboda, *Teachable Spirit*, 37.

15. Swoboda, *Teachable Spirit*, 47–48.

that they've done their homework. They know their field, and, given all the evidence, they've come to educated conclusions on various topics, so we should respect what they're saying and not simply dismiss it. Trusting experts means acknowledging that their voices bear significant weight in the public discourse.

Manipulating Public Perceptions

With an overabundance of information, people in power can sometimes abuse how experts are publicly received. By elevating unsubstantiated counterarguments, politicians today frequently employ anti-expert and anti-intellectual rhetoric, bashing experts and casting doubt on those who challenge their political goals. They might say things like, "Forget the fancy theories of the cultural elite—we need action!" This strategy is used to sway public perceptions on a subject and to trample dissenting voices, even those voices that are informed and well-supported. Philosopher Lee McIntyre sees a seven-step pattern that authoritarian political orders use to deceive, exploit, and manipulate their constituents:

1. The leader raises questions about an outlandish matter.
2. The leader provides no real evidence beyond their own conviction.
3. The leader states that the media isn't reliable because it is biased.
4. The people begin to doubt the press or at least see the matter as "controversial."
5. The people are uncertain, so they double down on their ideology and choose what fits their already held beliefs.
6. The political order proliferates fake news to reinforce steps 1–5.
7. Belief turns tribal, and the people believe the leader just because the leader said it.[16]

16. McIntyre, *Post-Truth*, 115.

This playbook promotes the distrust of media that's supposed to broadcast the news of current events, and it also bypasses the voices that would otherwise be seen as authorities in public discourse.

In the past, authorities were those who held expertise and were consistent in their guidance. Over time, they earned a reputation for integrity, sound judgment, and dependability. People learned to trust their opinions, even if they didn't always see eye to eye with them. It was like trusting Albert Einstein, a brilliant scientist, on social issues that pertained to science, such as nuclear disarmament. Or like having faith in Desmond Tutu, a South African religious leader and anti-apartheid advocate, for his moral insight. Yet even the most trusted people had their critics. Public authority wasn't about everyone loving you; it was about being seen as credible, serious, and ethical by most people despite their feelings toward them.

But in a post-truth era, experts—not just media spin-doctors—are frequently doubted and maligned. For instance, at the start of the COVID-19 pandemic, many people looked up to figures like Dr. Tedros Adhanom Ghebreyesus, the director-general of the World Health Organization (WHO), and Dr. Anthony Fauci, the director of the National Institute of Allergy and Infectious Diseases (NIAID) since 1984 and a health adviser for seven US presidents. However, as the pandemic continued, mixed messages—sometimes due to shifting scientific understandings and other times due to political agendas—caused a lot of people to lose trust in them. Social media distortions about vaccines, masks, and the virus's origins spread like wildfire, often painting experts like these as either corrupt or incompetent, even though they were simply trying to adapt to new scientific evidence. A large part of what caused the public's distrust of these experts was the flexible manipulation of truth by populist leaders via modern political lying.

In this world, well-educated politicians, power brokers, and influence peddlers master the trends of media consumption to sway and even manipulate the public. They create doubt about experts to influence our perceptions of reality. Instead of receiving news and learning from credible experts, we're served up versions of events that have been carefully crafted. Too often, these stories are not grounded in reality but are shaped by subjective viewpoints intended to appeal to our desires or to bolster someone else's political aspirations.

Power and Pragmatism in a Post-Truth Era

The way those in power spin and sell facts to the public reveals that many of our politicians have embraced a pragmatic approach to truth and morality.[17] Broadly speaking, **pragmatism** is a philosophical tradition that evaluates belief in terms of success and practical application. Instead of focusing on abstract ideals, pragmatism considers things to be true or right if they work in practice. Both the correspondence theorist (discussed earlier) and the pragmatist believe the statement "Water boils at 212 degrees Fahrenheit" is true, but for different reasons. For the correspondence theorist, the truth of the statement is fixed and independent of our use of the fact. For the pragmatist, the statement is true because it is proven to be useful and reliable. While the former believes water boils at 212 degrees Fahrenheit because that statement corresponds to a fact of reality, the latter believes it is true because it consistently works in practice. Since pragmatists deal with belief, they also view and test morality through real-life situations. But rather than viewing ethics as a rigid set of unchanging rules, pragmatists see it as a dynamic process shaped by human experiences, outcomes, and social norms. All in all, pragmatism is less a theory and more a philosophical approach to belief and meaning-making.

Pragmatist philosopher Sami Pihlström argues that such an approach to belief has, to a degree, unwittingly fueled our post-truth era. He believes that pragmatists like himself should recognize how the utilitarian view that truth is something useful has led in part to the fragmentation of truth in today's power-driven populist

17. Pragmatism was founded in the late 1800s by philosopher C. S. Peirce (1839–1914) and was subsequently popularized by philosopher and psychologist William James (1842–1910) and philosopher and social theorist John Dewey (1859–1952).

politics.[18] When truth is seen as only that which is expedient for our thinking,[19] it can be used to serve our motives. Truth, in this sense, does not guide our motives but works subserviently to help us achieve what we desire. However, this sort of political, populist pragmatism is what Pihlström calls a **vulgar pragmatism**—a pragmatism that's post-factualist and blurs the lines between truth and falsehood to serve the interests of those in power.[20] It's a superficial use of pragmatist ideas that's only motivated by self-interest,[21] like when a politician flip-flops on issues to get votes but consequently contradicts themselves. Or when a politician disregards truth for effectiveness. Such a politician might say, "Whether it's true or not, it got people talking!"

This is akin to what twentieth-century philosopher Hannah Arendt terms **modern political lying**—a systematic, ideologically driven form of dishonesty that fabricates new realities. While lying has always been a part of politics, modern political lying is not just occasional but systematic.[22] In the past, if someone told a single lie, others would easily be able to fact-check it against empirically verified facts that have shaped our collective understanding of reality. Modern political lying, however, does not exist within the normal boundaries of established truths. Rather, it crafts its own ideologically driven sense of reality and then communicates "alternative facts"[23] that correspond

18. Sami Pihlström, *Pragmatist Truth in the Post-Truth Age: Sincerity, Normativity, and Humanism* (Cambridge University Press, 2021), 1.

19. This is something philosopher William James famously said. See William James, *Pragmatism: A New Name for Some Old Ways of Thinking* (Longmans, Green, 1907), 222.

20. Pihlström, *Pragmatist Truth*, 13.

21. Pihlström believes the best antidote for vulgar pragmatism is to reconsider truth in a robust pragmatist way, viewing truth, truthfulness, and the acknowledgment of otherness as necessary for shaping our beliefs. See Pihlström, *Pragmatist Truth*, 19.

22. Hannah Arendt, *Crises of the Republic* (Harcourt, Brace, 1972), 4.

23. The term "alternative facts" was first used by Kellyanne Conway, a senior adviser to Donald Trump, during a 2017 interview on *Meet the Press*. She was backing up Sean Spicer, the White House press secretary, who had made false claims about the crowd size at Trump's inauguration. See Marilyn Wedge, "The Historical Origin of 'Alternative Facts,'" *Psychology Today*, January 23, 2017, https://www.psychologytoday.com/us/blog/suffer-the-children/201701/the-historical-origin-alternative-facts.

with a different narrative. Thus, modern political lying can only exist in a culture of lies that has been adopted by a group of people.[24]

Arendt says that people are willing to believe modern political lies because they cater toward what the population wants to hear. She writes, "Lies are often much more plausible, more appealing to reason, than reality, since the liar has the great advantage of knowing beforehand what the audience wishes or expects to hear. He has prepared his story for public consumption with a careful eye to making it credible, whereas reality has the disconcerting habit of confronting us with the unexpected, for which we were not prepared."[25] Rather than speaking truth to a reality, modern political liars craft stories that tickle people's ears in order to push their own agendas.

Reinforcing the desires of people for political expediency isn't anything new. In the Old Testament, we often see a clash between those who say what's publicly convenient and true prophets who faithfully say what God has revealed to them (e.g., 1 Kings 18; Isa. 30:9–11; Jer. 28; Ezek. 13; Amos 7:10–17). The false prophets echo what their leaders and the public want to hear, while the true prophets stand alone, face backlash, and speak uncomfortable truths that challenge the status quo.

A classic example of this is the story of the prophet Micaiah in 1 Kings 22. King Ahab of Israel wants to go to war against Ramoth-gilead and invites King Jehoshaphat of Judah to join him. Jehoshaphat wants to check in with God first, so Ahab brings in four hundred prophets who all say the same thing: "Go up, for the LORD will give it into the hand of the king" (v. 6). The prophets tell Ahab what he wants to hear, promising victory and divine backing. Jehoshaphat insists on hearing from another prophet of Yahweh, so Ahab reluctantly calls in Micaiah, who never prophesied good things for Ahab (v. 8). Micaiah starts off by mocking the king, mimicking

24. Lisa Stenmark, "Modern Political Lying: Science and Religion as Critical Discourse in a Post-Truth World," in *Navigating Post-Truth and Alternative Facts: Religion and Science as Political Theology*, ed. Jennifer Baldwin (Lexington Books, 2018), 6.

25. Arendt, *Crises of the Republic*, 6–7.

the false prophets by telling him to "go up and triumph" (v. 15), but when pressed, Micaiah shares a vision: "I saw all Israel scattered on the mountains like sheep that have no shepherd, and the LORD said, 'These have no master; let each one go home in peace'" (v. 17). Micaiah then reveals a heavenly scene where a spirit volunteers to be a lying spirit in the mouths of Ahab's prophets. Ahab, of course, brushes off Micaiah's warning and goes into battle, even disguising himself to avoid being targeted. But in the end, he is killed, proving Micaiah's prophecy right.

Has a lying spirit entered our mouths in this post-truth era? As Christians, do we reinforce the desires of the people or the delusions of our leaders to maintain a status quo? Are we complicit with their ungodly schemes? These are crucial questions that should guide our media interactions today.

While there's more to discuss about this era's relationship to truth and the media, so far, I've sketched out the basic post-truth context we live in. This context enables the rapid spread of mis- and disinformation, which we'll explore next, before wrapping up this chapter with some guidelines for hearing God amid our messy, post-truth reality.

Misinformation, Disinformation, and the Cheapening of Truth

Do you remember the whole "pizzagate" debacle? It started as a fringe conspiracy theory but ended up sparking real-life events, demonstrating how dangerous disinformation can be. In the weeks leading up to the 2016 US presidential election, WikiLeaks dropped a massive trove of emails from John Podesta, who was presidential candidate Hillary Clinton's campaign chair. Internet sleuths started digging through the emails hoping to find hidden truths. Innocent but oddly frequent mentions of pizza in Podesta's messages caught the eye of conspiracy theorists. They thought "pizza" was a code word for a secret pedophilia ring run by powerful Democrats. The theory grew on sites like 4chan and Reddit until proponents identified what they believed to be the epicenter of the alleged child-trafficking operation: Comet

Ping Pong, a trendy pizza place in Washington, DC, that doubles as a concert venue and a place to play ping-pong.

Fringe media influencers lent credibility to the theory, appealing to those already skeptical of the media and political figures. Then, on December 4, 2016, Edgar Maddison Welch, a twenty-eight-year-old father of two,[26] drove from North Carolina to Washington, DC, armed with an AR-15, looking to "investigate" the conspiracy himself. Families inside the restaurant hid in fear as he fired his weapon. Luckily, no one was hurt. When police apprehended him, he was shocked to discover there were no children or secret dungeons; there wasn't even a basement.[27]

This "pizzagate" tomfoolery illustrates how random clues, fallacious reasoning, and confirmation bias can lead to real-world threats. It shows us how manipulated narratives and viral content can blur the lines between entertainment, activism, and radicalization. And it shows us, unfortunately, how easily truth can be overshadowed by disinformed outrage in an age of algorithms.

Mis- and Disinformation

Sometimes people use the terms "misinformation" and "disinformation" interchangeably, but the main difference between the two lies in the intent behind the spread of false information. **Misinformation** refers to the sharing of false information without the goal of deceiving anyone, while **disinformation** involves the spreading of falsehoods for the purpose of misleading people. For example, when your uncle shares a story but gets some facts wrong, like the location where everything went down, he's unintentionally spreading misinformation. He really believes what he's saying and isn't trying to deceive anyone. On the other hand, disinformation is when someone

26. Adam Goldman, "The Comet Ping Pong Gunman Answers Our Reporter's Questions," *New York Times*, December 7, 2016, https://www.nytimes.com/2016/12/07/us/edgar-welch-comet-pizza-fake-news.html.

27. "The Saga of 'Pizzagate': The Fake Story That Shows How Conspiracy Theories Spread," BBC News, December 2, 2016, https://www.bbc.com/news/blogs-trending-38156985.

deliberately twists the truth to manipulate how others perceive a person or situation. It's like when a politician casts doubt on and tarnishes a rival's reputation for personal benefit. Even if it's later proven that the politician's claims were false, the harm has already been done because people now view the opponent through a lens of distrust.

Social media algorithms are filled with both mis- and disinformation. As mentioned above, algorithms focus on engagement, not accuracy. When any given content sparks outrage, fear, or excitement, the algorithm thinks, "Awesome! Let's show some more of that!" It doesn't care about the factual accuracy; it only looks at how well the content performs. Misinformation spreads quickly because regular users share what they *think* is true, like a bogus health tip or a misreported statistic, often out of genuine concern. Disinformation, on the other hand, flourishes when bad actors—like trolls, bots, review bombers, or political teams—try to manipulate the system. Disinformation campaigns create emotionally charged lies that are designed to provoke strong reactions and go viral.[28] And once something goes viral, mis- and disinformation gets endlessly recycled as it decisively enters our public discourse.

For a time, starting around the mid-2010s, social media outlets sought to fight against the spread of mis- and disinformation by adding independent fact-checkers. This was mainly due to growing public and political pressure after significant events where mis- and disinformation caused social turmoil[29]—like when the FBI confirmed there was Russian interference in the 2016 US presidential election.[30] With a foreign nation meddling in US politics, government and watchdog

28. Killian McLoughlin and William Brady, "Human-Algorithm Interactions Help Explain the Spread of Misinformation," *Current Opinion in Psychology* 56 (April 2024), https://www.sciencedirect.com/science/article/abs/pii/S2352250X23002154?via%3Dihub.

29. Chenyan Jia and Taeyoung Lee, "Journalistic Interventions Matter: Understanding How Americans Perceive Fact-Checking Labels," *Harvard Kennedy School Misinformation Review* 5, no. 2 (2024): 2.

30. See Special Counsel Robert Mueller III's report: "Report on the Investigation into Russian Interference in the 2016 Presidential Election," U.S. Department of Justice (March 2019), https://www.justice.gov/archives/sco/file/1373816/dl.

groups called for accountability. To show they were serious about being fair and to avoid more regulations, social media platforms brought in nonpartisan independent fact-checkers. By collaborating with third-party organizations like Snopes, PolitiFact, and the International Fact-Checking Network, the platforms aimed to steer clear of being seen as biased or as gatekeepers of truth.

However, right around the time of the 2024 US presidential election, some platforms began quietly scaling back or even scrapping their fact-checking efforts, often without much public explanation.[31] By then, fact-checking had become a hot-button political issue. Some users, particularly on the right, accused social media platforms of bias or censorship, especially throughout the pandemic and during election seasons.[32] Companies were also worried about being seen as editorializing content.

Ideologically, some fact-checking opponents subscribe to what political theorist Langdon Winner calls cyber libertarianism, "a collection of ideas that links ecstatic enthusiasm for electronically mediated forms of living with radical, right-wing libertarian ideas about the proper definition of freedom, social life, economics, and politics in the years to come."[33] Elon Musk's vision for social media appears to align with cyber libertarianism, especially after he bought Twitter, now X. He refers to himself as a "free speech maximalist," believing that all speech should be allowed unless it breaks the law. In this view, social media should be like a public town square with minimal rules on what people can say online.[34] The idea is that by allowing more speech, it can help counteract harmful or negative speech, and that

31. "Meta Drops Fact-Checking on Instagram, Facebook," PBS, January 10, 2025, https://www.pbs.org/newshour/classroom/daily-news-lessons/2025/01/meta-drops-fact-checking-on-social-media-sites.

32. Brian Fung, "How Republicans Pushed Social Media Companies to Stop Fighting Election Misinformation," CNN, October 21, 2024, https://www.cnn.com/2024/10/21/politics/election-social-media-misinformation-republicans.

33. Langdon Winner, "Cyberlibertarian Myths and the Prospects for Community," *Computers and Society* 27, no. 3 (1997): 14–19.

34. Elizabeth Dwoskin, "Elon Musk Wants a Free Speech Utopia. Technologists Clap Back," *Washington Post*, April 18, 2022, https://www.washingtonpost.com/technology/2022/04/18/musk-twitter-free-speech/.

over time, people will filter out nonsense and highlight the truth. Musk has pushed for X's Community Notes as a way to crowdsource fact-checking,[35] but crowdsourcing is prone to being manipulated and can't keep up with viral misinformation.[36]

Can we really trust that people will let the truth prevail? Experience seems to show us the opposite: Truth will be subjected to power. Just so, Musk's cyber libertarianism has caused many new problems. It has invited harmful speech, violent rhetoric, and mis- and disinformation to rejoin public discourse. If a person lacks the critical thinking skills to separate fact from fiction, we might see reactions of confusion, chaos, or even harm. Free speech does not mean we can say whatever we want without consequences. In a modern society, we still have social responsibilities toward each other when we enjoy our freedom of speech. Even as we exercise our rights, our free speech shouldn't cheapen our sense of truth.

The Kitschification of Truth

What does it look like when a society's sense of truth is cheapened? According to Botz-Bornstein, the West has slowly become more and more "decultured": It's becoming homogenized, and its cultural values are being continually denigrated. People need something to believe in, and historically, **cultures**—broadly understood as the collective lifestyles shaped by language, traditions, religions, art, and shared histories—have been essential for conveying meaning and establishing worldviews.[37] But in our current global environment, "truth is increasingly produced instantaneously without cultural mediation."[38] We state our own truths in ways that resonate with

35. Kate Conger, "Meta Turns to Community Notes, Mirroring X," *New York Times*, January 7, 2025, https://www.nytimes.com/2025/01/07/business/meta-community-notes-x.html.

36. Will Oremus, Trisha Thadani, and Jeremy Merrill, "Elon Musk Says X Users Fight Falsehoods. The Falsehoods Are Winning," *Washington Post*, October 30, 2024, https://www.washingtonpost.com/technology/2024/10/30/elon-musk-x-fact-check-community-notes-misinformation/.

37. Botz-Bornstein, *New Aesthetics of Deculturation*, 2.

38. Botz-Bornstein, *New Aesthetics of Deculturation*, 2.

us personally, without engaging our shared communities or cultures to make or convey meaning. Societies become decultured when rich, communal ways of finding meaning are stripped away and replaced by superficial values that cater to our own tastes. Botz-Bornstein correlates this deculturation with the art term **kitsch**, which means art that is considered cheap, tasteless, or overly sentimental. Kitsch is art that's too flashy, cheesy, or over-the-top. It tries hard to be beautiful or to evoke feeling but comes off as fake. Think of mass-produced paintings of sad puppies or bobblehead Jesus figurines. For Botz-Bornstein, how one comes to know the truth, and truth itself, has been "kitschified."

In a decultured society, shallow ethical values emerge as uncritical fundamentalisms, even as empty aesthetic values take shape as kitsch. In both instances, a simplistic approach to value fills the void left by rich, culturally developed meanings. When individual freedom is valued above everything else, the result is a decultured, narcissistic view of life where the self becomes the sole reference point for meaning. This self-centered authority also influences what people in a society consider to be true.

Botz-Bornstein suggests that alternative truths emerge not from misinformation but from a "kitschification" of truth.[39] He says our current era shouldn't just be seen as one filled with outright lies but as a time when truths are oversimplified and misrepresented. The kitschification of truth involves people presenting and believing distorted versions of reality as if such fabrications were genuine. In other words, people come to trust the culture of lies they inhabit. Fundamentally, kitschification is the cheapening of truth—making it something vacuous and small. Throughout modernity, truth has been reduced to facts and empirical evidence, but in our decultured society today, "truth" has become nothing more than a tool used to persuade people. It is politicized and used pragmatically.

Dudiak agrees with Botz-Bornstein, suggesting that our ongoing crisis of truth is caused by an impoverished sense of the term; it

39. Botz-Bornstein, *New Aesthetics of Deculturation*, 12.

is "too narrow, too emaciated, too weak, and too fragile to support the weight that we of necessity place upon truth."[40] It's weak because it's cheap. It can't handle the existential and theological issues that keep us up at night. We ask why we should do certain things, and our distorted sense of truth responds, "To get what you want." But we know there is more to life than this shallow self-indulgence. Truth—real truth—beckons us to more. Just as Dietrich Bonhoeffer pointed out the difference between **cheap grace**—grace that's given freely but requires nothing of us—and authentic, **costly grace** that requires a person to give up their old life and commit fully to Christ in discipleship,[41] we can also differentiate between cheap truth and authentic truth. **Cheap truth** is the "truth" of the post-truth era, a counterfeit that's based on emotion and personal preferences, lacks accountability, and is wielded for personal gain. In contrast, **authentic truth** is truth as faithfulness, truth that promises to live in a way that is true.[42] But while Botz-Bornstein wants our society to reembrace a culturally mediated sense of truth, Dudiak sees "truth as faithfulness" as the richer view of truth that's expressed in the Bible.[43] Truth is not that which is mediated by a broader culture but that which is expressed in Scripture and mediated by the church.

Truth as faithfulness goes beyond the correspondence theory of truth. It's not merely stating a fact or expressing a single moment of truth; it's an ongoing commitment to truth over time. It's about *being* true, not just about saying the right words. When two people vow to be faithful in their marriage, they're committing to a future that lasts until death. Saying "I promise to be faithful" is a commitment to live out a truth that extends into the future. Truth as faithfulness is not based on facts but on a promise—and it's choosing to make that promise true every day, no matter the circumstances.[44]

40. Dudiak, *Post-Truth?*, 9.
41. Dietrich Bonhoeffer, *The Cost of Discipleship* (Touchstone, 1995), 45.
42. Dudiak, *Post-Truth?*, 40.
43. Dudiak, *Post-Truth?*, 14.
44. Dudiak, *Post-Truth?*, 12.

Hearing God's Truth

Feeling a bit anxious by this post-truth chaos? I know I am! Stepping into a post-truth reality feels like entering a house of mirrors built by George Orwell himself. The echoes of *1984* are hard to ignore. We're surrounded by screens—small ones in our pockets, huge ones in public spaces, and even invisible, algorithmic ones that watch us while pretending to entertain us. They subtly deliver carefully crafted messages until we forget what's real. Our "Ministry of Truth" doesn't need to burn books; it simply buries them under a mountain of social media content. Our "Thought Police" pressures us through reactions and emojis, and we're not just watched by "Big Brother"; we willingly follow him. The scariest part is that we've gotten used to it. We've become accomplices. We catch ourselves nodding along to things that once sent shivers down our spines. We scroll past obvious lies because confronting them feels exhausting and pointless. This new (un)reality is not temporary—it's a constant, intangible presence. So what can we do? What would it mean to discern the Spirit through this messy situation?

If we reframe our thinking and adopt Dudiak's concept of "truth as faithfulness," we can start getting to the core of what it means to be faithful and true followers of Christ in a post-truth world. We'll shift our focus from the albatross of manipulation and re-center our hearts and minds on the things of God. While circumstances were different in the first century, Paul encourages the church in Philippi to re-center their hearts and minds as well: "Finally, brothers and sisters, whatever is true, whatever is honorable, whatever is just, whatever is pure, whatever is pleasing, whatever is commendable, if there is any excellence and if there is anything worthy of praise, think about these things" (Phil. 4:8). Following Paul's advice to the early church, hearing God in our post-truth era also entails giving ear to the things that are true, honorable, just, pure, pleasing, commendable, excellent, and worthy of praise. When we do that, we allow ourselves to be formed by what is godly instead of what is manipulative. But if the post-truth era is so pervasive and inescapable, how can we even tell what the godly things are? Can we discern when a lying spirit has entered the mouths we listen to?

As discussed in the last chapter, the spiritual practice of prayerful Scripture reading can help us stay focused on what matters in a post-truth era. But first, let's look at two practical and broadly applicable tips that can help us recognize if we're being duped: screening for authenticity and thinking critically.

Screening for Authenticity

In some ways, authenticity is the foundation of truth. Not only does authenticity imply that we are true to our own nature; it also means we believe that what we represent actually corresponds to reality.

As I've discussed above, falsehoods can spread faster than facts, and the lines between fact and fiction are so blurred by emotionalism and disinformation that it's nearly impossible to tell what's what. Amid this, authenticity takes on an important discerning role for us today: It's an early screen for truth. That doesn't mean authentic belief is equivalent to what's true—somebody can authentically believe something and still be wrong. Rather, it means that if someone legitimately believes what they say and lives it out, we'll give them a shot. On the other hand, we hate hypocrisy and double standards because they point to inauthenticity; they reveal when someone doesn't actually believe or live what they're saying. Just as our spam filters discard suspicious emails from our inboxes, we can be immediately suspicious when someone says something they don't believe. If it's not real to them, why should it be real to us?

This should tell us something about our Christian witness. If we don't act like Jesus, why should anyone trust us when we say Jesus is our Lord? While we are saved through faith by God's grace, what we do and how we live in the world prove that we're authentic followers of Jesus (James 2:18). As Jesus so poignantly reminds his disciples, "By this everyone will know that you are my disciples, if you have love for one another" (John 13:35). For Jesus, authentic Christianity is proven by the way Christians love one another. This is how Jesus has called us to reflect him in the public square.

Thinking Critically

While authenticity is important in our era, it must be accompanied by critical thinking. A conspiracy theorist might genuinely think a claim is true, but if their belief is based on unsubstantiated claims about reality and doesn't have solid reasoning behind it, then it doesn't hold up as valid.

Many years ago, one of my college professors gave our class a handout titled "The Rules of Academic Discourse." It laid out some steps to follow when doing academic work, making sure we approach opposing views critically but generously. The first point stated that before we criticize a viewpoint, we need to fully understand it. This sounds straightforward, but much of the misguided content on social media doesn't accurately represent the views that are challenged. To really know if we understand the opposing side, we should express it in a way that its supporters would agree with. Only then can we offer critique, pointing out where the argument might be misinformed, inconsistent, illogical, or biased. Even then, we should look for areas where the opposing view is partially right in order to highlight what remains valuable about it. I've followed these rules throughout my academic career, and I'm a better scholar today because of it.

Not long ago, I had a chance to test these rules. A student shared with me a video she found on YouTube from a well-known Christian YouTuber who was questioning the appearance of a Catholic ceremony. In the video, this content creator was appalled by what she saw, even going so far as to claim that the Catholic church was engaging in idol worship and opening a door for demonic influence. I shared the academic discourse handout with my student, and then we rewatched the video, pausing frequently to discuss the YouTuber's points. As we did so, my student quickly began to realize that this person was misinformed and biased, without a clear understanding of what the Catholic ceremony was about or of the meaning behind the symbols being used. Instead, she was jumping to conclusions based on appearances and making harsh judgments. While the YouTuber seemed confident, a little bit of scrutiny revealed just how wrong she was. This scenario shows how important critical thinking is when assessing the validity of a source. The problem is that most nineteen-year-olds don't have theologian friends at hand to ask questions about fishy YouTube content. So what can we do?

The other day, I was chatting with a colleague about this very issue, and she asked me if there were any criteria for critical thinking like there are for theology. Perhaps there was a Wesleyan Quadrilateral, but for critical thought? The Wesleyan Quadrilateral identifies four sources of authority for theological reflection: reason, tradition, experience, and Scripture. Scripture is the central source, and the other three are interpretive aids. While I haven't yet found an official "critical discourse quadrilateral," philosopher Craig Boyd does pinpoint three criteria to look for in a valued expert who offers opinion: (1) They should be well-educated in the relevant field, (2) they should be recognized as an expert by other experts in the field, and (3) they should have experience submitting their work for the review of other experts.[45] This is the sort of criteria that's used in academia across every field. In fact, to get published in an academic peer-reviewed journal, at least two scholars in the field have to do a blind review of the submission. There is, ideally, minimal bias at play in academia. You can generally tell if someone is a credible source if they have been deemed credible by other experts in the field. Hence, Boyd's criteria can screen out people who, like the YouTuber, might look the part but don't actually know what they're talking about.

While authenticity screens and criteria for critical discourse can help us discern what's true or false in a post-truth era, we should remember that because discernment is fundamentally a spiritual practice, we must rely on the Holy Spirit to hear and be led by God's truth.

45. Craig Boyd, "Making America Humble Again: Humility and Magnanimity as Greatness in a Post-Veridical World," in *Navigating Post-Truth and Alternative Facts: Religion and Science as Political Theology*, ed. Jennifer Baldwin (Lexington Books, 2018), 55.

The last chapter highlighted how a spiritual reading of Scripture should be fully entrenched in God's story and how contemplative reading allows us to absorb what the Spirit is revealing through the text. But I'd argue that we can also see Spirit-led, contemplative Scripture reading as an antidote to the spiritual and emotional anxieties brought about by the post-truth nonsense that floods our feeds daily.

In his handbook *The Scripture Practice*, evangelical pastor John Mark Comer says the digital age has "rewired our brains" to adapt to a clickbait mode of reading the Bible that's designed for rapid consumption of fragmented, sensationalized headlines.[46] Since clickbait reading provokes emotional reactions and dopamine hits, imagine reading Scripture this way! We scour the pages of the Bible (or the hits of a Google search) for proof texts that confirm our own bias. We twist passages to mean whatever we want them to mean. Algorithms already reflect us, so why shouldn't Scripture do the same? I've witnessed clickbait Scripture readings used to justify wars, greed, sexual misconduct, and hate—the very things Jesus stood against and that foster a carnal spirituality that's far from Christian.

Conversely, spiritual readings of Scripture are slow and reflective. They're not consumptive but involve listening to God's still small voice (1 Kings 19:12 NKJV) as we internalize revelations about God and the things God cares about. This sort of reading is a spiritual discipline that becomes "a way of meeting God on every page and opening your spirit to his Spirit to heal and change you from the inside out."[47] But while we read Scripture contemplatively for spiritual formation, we should also study Scripture to ensure that we understand what it says. This means praying before and after reading a text, asking the Spirit to reveal whatever God wants us to know. It means reading slowly and repeatedly and maybe looking at different translations of the Bible. It means making observations about the text, asking questions like, Who's speaking? Who's the audience? What's actually happening in the passage? Are there repeated words

46. John Mark Comer, *The Scripture Practice: A Four-Session Guide to Reading the Bible as an Apprentice of Jesus* (WaterBrook, 2025), 43.

47. Comer, *Scripture Practice*, 4.

or references to other passages in the text? It means consulting commentaries and biblical dictionaries to get a sense of the context. It might mean consulting the original Greek or Hebrew of a word to better catch its meaning. It means meditating on God's words, finding ways to apply them in our lives, and then putting them into action by living them out. Hearing God in Scripture requires prayer, critical insight, and a receptive spirit.

Just as academics engage opposing views critically and generously to show understanding of the arguments, we should study Scripture to make sure we understand it. But rather than checking for flaws in the logic of the Bible, we must recognize that God is actually talking to us through Scripture. Because of this, as we study Scripture, we learn to check for inconsistencies in our faith. Do our views of society and our public actions reflect who Jesus is and what he cares about, as revealed in Scripture? Is there anything in what we believe or in the ways we live that's misinformed, inconsistent, illogical, or biased? As these past two chapters have discussed, studying Scripture in order to love God more and be formed into Christ's image is a spiritual practice.[48] It entails letting Scripture teach us and lead us toward correction and reproof (2 Tim. 3:16). When we read Scripture this way, we join David when he prays,

> Search me, O God, and know my heart;
> test me and know my thoughts.
> See if there is any wicked way in me,
> and lead me in the way everlasting. (Ps. 139:23–24)

The era of algorithms can push us toward a faith that's too reduced, too easy. As we allow the Spirit to search our hearts and Scripture to correct us, we must ask if our faith has become shallow rather than simple. A simple faith is uncorrupted and solely about being a witness of God's love in the world as we are spiritually formed in Christ. A shallow faith, on the other hand, is narcissistic and mostly

48. Comer, *Scripture Practice*, 63.

about us feeling happy or fulfilled. We must also ask if our faith has become cheap rather than charitable. A charitable faith considers how Christ in us can be a blessing to others. A cheap faith only cares about what we can get out of it. Finally, we must ask if our faith has become harsh rather than honest. An honest faith is willing to sit with the tough issues as a means for seeking Christ. A harsh faith simplifies truth to mere facts and uses those facts as a barometer to judge others. This type of faith kitschifies truth and weaponizes Scripture against others. In a world that listens to nonsense and promotes what's shallow, cheap, and harsh, let's hear God and demonstrate a faith that's simple, charitable, and honest.

Conclusion

I've always been struck with Jesus saying "truly, truly" before he drops a truth bomb on somebody. While he says "truly, I say to you" many times throughout the Gospels, the double affirmation of "truly, truly" is unique to the Gospel of John, where Jesus says it a whopping twenty-five times! The word Jesus uses for "truly" is the Greek word for "amen" (ἀμήν), which means "surely" or "verily." Jesus uses this double amen whenever he's trying to emphasize a point. It's like in American slang when someone asks, "Are you for real?" and you respond, "Like, *for real* for real." Whenever Jesus starts a sentence with "truly, truly," we know that something's about to go down! If even Jesus had to use a double amen to be taken seriously, then maybe we shouldn't take it personally when we have to prove our claims in a post-truth era. I guess it was okay, then, that my student did a Google search to fact-check what I said in class; his action said more about the times we live in than about my integrity as a teacher.

Discernment in a pluralistic and misinformed age means tuning into the Spirit and hearing the voice of Jesus. Hearing God requires knowing his character and what he cares about, both of which are revealed to us by the Spirit as we enter into prayer and participate in Spirit-led Scripture reading. Discernment also means paying attention to the times we're in. We've spent a lot of time this chapter "reading the newspaper," so to speak, and have discovered that our post-truth reality confronts us with never-before-seen challenges for hearing God. A major part of discernment is identifying these challenges and learning how to live faithfully and truthfully in spite of them. This chapter concludes part 1 of this book, which focused on hearing God. Next, we'll explore what it means to follow Jesus in this pluralistic and misinformed age. Hearing God and following the Spirit go together, which is evidenced by what Jesus said in John 10:27: "My sheep hear my voice. I know them, and they follow me." May we hear his voice clearly.

KEY WORDS

- **authentic truth**: Truth as faithfulness; truth that promises to live in a way that is true
- **cheap grace**: Grace that's given freely but requires nothing of us
- **cheap truth**: A counterfeit truth that's based on emotion and personal preferences, that lacks accountability, and is wielded for personal gain
- **confirmation bias**: When people look for, interpret, and recall information that corroborates their existing beliefs
- **correspondence theory of truth**: The idea that truth is in accord with reality or facts
- **costly grace**: Grace that requires a person to give up their old life and commit fully to Christ in discipleship
- **culture**: The collective lifestyle of a group of people shaped by language, traditions, religions, art, and shared histories
- **disinformation**: The spreading of falsehoods with the purpose of misleading people
- **kitsch**: Art that is considered cheap, tasteless, or too sentimental
- **misinformation**: The sharing of false information without the goal of deceiving anyone

- **modern political lying**: A systematic, ideologically driven form of dishonesty that fabricates new realities
- **news pundits**: Subject-area experts who are brought in to give opinions about current events
- **post-truth era**: A cultural environment where facts hold less power in influencing public opinion than emotional appeals or personal convictions
- **pragmatism**: A philosophical tradition that evaluates belief in terms of success and practical application
- **social media algorithms**: The rules that determine what we see when we log into social media apps
- **truth**: That which is in line with what's real or factual
- **vulgar pragmatism**: A post-factualist pragmatism that blurs the lines between truth and falsehood to serve the interests of those in power

DISCUSSION QUESTIONS

- Where do you get your news? Do you find it difficult to trust newscasters and pundits? Why?
- What sources do you use to evaluate truth claims? Do you have any screening criteria that help you determine if something is misinformation (or disinformation)?
- How often do you slow down to study Scripture for spiritual formation? What can you do differently in your life to prioritize Spirit-led Scripture reading?

REFLECTION EXERCISE

Choose one day this week to turn off all notifications and practice digital silence. On that day, set aside three ten-minute periods for listening prayer. Ask, "God, what are you saying today?"

Part 2

Following the Spirit

four

Following the Spirit Past Political Tribalism

When I was six, my family made the big move from Germany to the US. I didn't really know much about America, just that it was the land of cowboys and Mickey Mouse. When my sister and I started grade school, most things felt pretty normal, but some things were vastly different. Schools in America were massive, kids took buses to school, and the boys' bathrooms had urinals in them. But the most noticeable difference for me was how patriotic schools in America were. In German classrooms, you won't see flags, and no one recites a pledge or sings a national anthem. This could be because of Germany's "culture of remembrance" that formed after the reunification between East and West Germany.[1] This culture created a national identity that would constantly acknowledge the horrors of World War II, accept responsibility, and consequently foster a new, non-nationalistic sense

1. Hans-Georg Moeller and Paul D'Ambrosio, *You and Your Profile: Identity After Authenticity* (Columbia University Press, 2021), 100.

of morality.[2] Symbols of nationalistic pride have been downplayed in Germany ever since.

I remember my first day at school in America. At 8:00 a.m. sharp my teacher and the entire class stood up. Everyone placed their hands over their hearts at once. Then the group recited, "I pledge allegiance to the flag of the United States of America." Everyone knew this from memory except me. I stood there, silent, wondering why everyone was doing this. We were venerating a flag as if it were Jesus. I couldn't figure out why we were pledging allegiance to a nationalizing symbol.

My sister told me that she felt the same way. In fact, she used to recite the pledge but would say instead, "I pledge allegiance *to God*." My solution wasn't so pious. Instead of pledging to God, I said, "I pledge allegiance to the flag of the United States of *Germany*." (I was six and barely knew English; don't judge me.)

Despite my weird loyalty to Germany, it seems something clicked for both my sister and me. We made our own pledges—not to America but to our own consciences. Out of principle, we recited a commitment to not blindly follow an institution. In time, we relaxed our stances. We grew into our new lives and became Americanized. Yet even now when I hear the pledge, a small part of me wants to mumble "to the United States of Germany."

I recount this story to talk about the complexities that exist when considering national identity and covenantal fidelity to the kingdom of God. Jesus said his kingdom does "not belong to this world" (John 18:36). It's a kingdom not formed by elections or borders but by sacrificial love and the Spirit of truth. Jesus's kingdom has endured persecutions, the fall of nations, and the silencing of empires. Yet it persists.

The Bible says the kingdom of God requires our *full* allegiance—we are either fully with God or fully with the world. As James 4:4 says, "Friendship with the world is enmity with God." In Scripture, the world is seen as a singular reality, as everything that opposes God's lordship. When we talk about political allegiances, we must remember

2. Moeller and D'Ambrosio, *You and Your Profile*, 101.

that earthly nations are *not* part of God's kingdom—they're part of the world. So why would we give our full allegiance to a worldly kingdom? To pledge allegiance to something is to allow it to name us, claim us, and incorporate us into its identity-forming system. And there are spiritual consequences to any such allegiance. As we discussed in chapter 1, many forces shape our identities, and national allegiances are no exception.

Identity is both internal and external, both personal and social—it's formed through the combined personal-psychological experience of selfhood and how this is expressed and viewed socially.[3] **Identity** is thus the way people and groups perceive and convey who they are in relation to social roles, relationships, and norms. When we're given a name, we're identified *as* something—we're seen as part of a tribe, culture, class, ethnicity, or another social group. Names define us and determine how we think of ourselves and present ourselves to others. With that being said, I believe this political season is so volatile because it's not just a clash of ideas but of identities.

Although the main point of this chapter is to talk about the spiritual dangers of political tribalism, the first part will set the stage through a discussion about identity, names, and labels. Because naming is so formative, we must resist the names and labels the world tries to put on us while also living into the names God has given us. Understanding this helps us to see how the political world plays games with our formation, labeling us, pitting us against each other, and ultimately malforming us into fearful and hateful pawns in some political regime's quest for power. The Spirit of Christ must instead be our foundational influence in shaping our identities as kingdom people. When we recognize this, we'll see that our worship of God alone allows us to collectively embrace our identities as members of God's family.

As the title suggests, this chapter will focus on *following* the Spirit. So, not only will we keep thinking about how to discern God's voice in a pluralistic and often misinformed age, but we'll also look at what

3. Moeller and D'Ambrosio, *You and Your Profile*, 205.

it means to act on what God's voice is telling us. What's the point of hearing God's voice clearly if we don't follow it? This chapter demonstrates how worship helps us walk straight ahead when political forces try to throw us off our paths, and the next chapter discusses what it means to keep moving forward during a crisis when the path ahead is hard to see. In each case, following the Spirit means being totally devoted to God and not being led astray by anything the world might offer, political or otherwise.

Power and Names

Giving something a name shapes its identity and meaning. In Genesis 2:19–20, God tells Adam to name all the animals. This is important for a few reasons: First, it highlights the unique role of humans in God's creation. We are the only ones who can reflect God's creative nature. Just like God created everything by saying "Let there be," humans also take part in this creative process by naming what God has made. It also indicates that humans have a divinely granted authority over creation—"dominion," as the Bible calls it (1:28)—but this doesn't mean we should dominate or devalue anything. Our authority comes from God, who governs us with the kindness of a loving father, and so we should mirror God's character by caring for the things we have authority over with love. Last, for Adam, naming things helped establish relationships and even highlighted what was missing. As Adam observed unity and companionship throughout creation, he realized he lacked a suitable partner. On a social level, naming helped organize God's creation, like a filing system, making it easier to see when any part of creation was lacking or in need of something.

All Powers and Dominion

Before we continue, I should clarify something: When I say there's power in naming something and when I mention the word "dominion," I am *not* talking about dominion theology. **Dominion theology** is a controversial theological viewpoint that asserts Christians should have authority or dominion over every sector of life, such as government, culture, law, and society. It stems from a specific, and I would argue poor, reading of Genesis 1:28.[4] The aim of dominion theology goes beyond matters of salvation and discipleship; it seeks to reshape society based on what is perceived as God's law. Christians are encouraged not just to spread the gospel but also to take charge, govern, and influence culture as part of their spiritual and moral responsibilities.[5]

I find this way of thinking incredibly problematic. It's infatuated with power, and those who follow it seem to think of themselves as God's power brokers.[6] Not only do they misinterpret the Genesis command of dominion as a call for conquest or control rather than stewardship, but they also seem to misunderstand what the kingdom of God actually is. At Jesus's trial, Pilate asked if Jesus was a national ruler, since he was given the title "King of the Jews." Jesus replied:

> "Do you ask this on your own, or did others tell you about me?" Pilate replied, "I am not a Jew, am I? Your own nation and the chief priests have handed you over to me. What have you done?" Jesus answered, "My kingdom does not belong to this world. If my kingdom belonged to this world, my followers would be fighting to keep me from being handed over to the Jews. But as it is, my kingdom is not from here." (John 18:34–36)

Jesus recognizes that the **kingdom of God**—the reality where Christ is king and the whole world is at shalom—stretches beyond space and time. **Shalom** is God's goal for creation: a life of peace, completeness, and holistic well-being.[7]

4. C. Peter Wagner, *Dominion! Your Role in Bringing Heaven to Earth* (Destiny Image, 2022), 64.

5. Wagner, *Dominion!*, 1.

6. Matthew Taylor, *The Violent Take It by Force: The Christian Movement That Is Threatening Our Democracy* (Broadleaf Books, 2024), 70.

7. I expanded on this concept in Steven Félix-Jäger, *The Problem and Promise of Freedom: A Public Theology for the Church* (Baker Academic, 2025), 16.

The church represents God's kingdom here on earth; we are ambassadors of king Jesus (2 Cor. 5:20). Our role is to bear witness to God's kingdom so it can take root in places and flourish. We're not like conquistadors seizing territory (even if the word "territory" is used metaphorically by dominionists to mean spiritual influence). Our task is to enact our divinely assigned mission of reconciliation (vv. 18–20), promoting shalom in the world. If you're involved in pastoral ministry, think about the harm that could arise from using dominion language for spiritual influence. How do your Native American or immigrant congregants feel when they hear people say things like "We're taking the land"? Such rhetoric is not only careless but also deeply unbiblical.

It's as if dominionists read Genesis 1:28, saw the word "dominion," interpreted it through a modern lens of power, and then filtered the rest of the Bible through that lens. But as we continue to read beyond Genesis, we see a very different story unfold. We see the fall, redemption, the empowered church, and the coming king. We see worldly notions of power being turned upside down through the story of Jesus's birth, his teachings, his death, and resurrection—and at Pentecost and throughout the book of Revelation. Time and time again, we see God triumph through weakness.

One of the most powerful images in the Bible appears in Revelation 5, where no one is deemed worthy to open the sealed scroll that chronicles everyone's fate. Then, an elder approaches and says, "Do not weep. See, the Lion of the tribe of Judah, the Root of David, has conquered, so that he can open the scroll and its seven seals" (v. 5). The conquering lion of Judah is the one strong enough to break the seal. But then the Bible completely subverts our common understanding of power! When everyone turns to see the mighty lion, they instead find a slaughtered lamb (v. 6). Jesus, through his death, conquers death. The lion triumphs *because* he is sacrificed as a lamb. After the lamb takes the scroll, the elders and living creatures sing:

> You are worthy to take the scroll
> and to break its seals,

for you were slaughtered and by your blood you ransomed for
God
saints from every tribe and language and people and
nation;
you have made them a kingdom and priests serving our God,
and they will reign on earth. (vv. 9–10)

This song says a lot. Jesus is our worthy Savior because it was he who was sacrificed. He alone is worthy to unveil the judgments contained in the scroll—only he can save, and only he can judge.

Jesus's kingdom consists of saints from every tribe, language, and nation. He commissioned his followers to go, baptize, and teach people (Matt. 28:18–20), not to take spiritual land or dominate sectors of life. If we remain true to our mission, the world around us will be transformed—not through forceful expansion but through grace. Our role is to faithfully show Jesus to others, and when they embrace Christ as their Savior, the Holy Spirit will work to heal and transform them from within.

The only one who could actually dominate anyone was and is Jesus, because he's God incarnate, the lion of Judah, and the worthy lamb. But Jesus doesn't exercise his authority that way. Instead, Jesus chooses to welcome children (Mark 10:13–16), feed the hungry (Matt. 14:13–21), heal the sick and outcasts (Mark 1:40–45), forgive sins (Luke 7:36–50), and even wash his disciples' feet (John 13:1–17). At the Last Supper, right after washing the disciples' feet, Jesus says, "So if I, your Lord and Teacher, have washed your feet, you also ought to wash one another's feet. For I have set you an example, that you also should do as I have done to you" (vv. 14–15). Jesus tells his disciples to serve others, not dominate them.

If folks hear the teachings of Jesus and witness his actions and end up with a dominion theology that encourages them to reclaim society through power, they've profoundly misunderstood Jesus. If you've found yourself influenced by dominion theology, as many of us have, I want to encourage you to stop for a moment and do some spiritual reading of Matthew 5:3–12. This is the opening to the Sermon on the Mount, Jesus's longest recorded teaching. You'll see, I believe, that Jesus calls us to lead by grace and humility, not by force. Read it slowly through lectio divina, and let the teachings of Christ sink into every fiber of your being.

Now that we've "eaten" some of the teachings of Christ, let's reconsider Jesus's relationship to power as evidenced by the cross. The cross of Christ shows that might doesn't determine what's right. The Bible tells us that Jesus could have called down legions of angels to save him from arrest and crucifixion (Matt. 26:53), but he chose not to. His crucifixion looked like defeat—he was overpowered by the Roman and Jewish leaders who used their might to silence him. Yet he rose again, showing that sacrificial love and obedience to God's will can overcome even the strongest forces in the world. Jesus's life, death, and resurrection ignited a first-century movement that spread globally, not through force and power but through love, gracious action, and the truth of the gospel. The early Christian church flourished despite persecution, proving that God works through the weak. We must live into this paradoxical truth: To be an authentic witness of Christ in a society that longs for truth, we do not need strength. We need weakness (2 Cor. 12:9–10).

When God invites us to name things, as Adam did, it's not about hoarding power or trying to dominate. Neither can we control things by virtue of naming them. Proverbs 18:21 says, "Death and life are in the power of the tongue, and those who love it will eat its fruits." While this verse definitely highlights the power of words, the Word of Faith movement takes it a step further, saying that spoken words have the power to create, similar to how God spoke everything into existence in Genesis 1. This goes far beyond joining God in the creative process to instead claim that we ourselves can wield power through naming.

This line of thinking, sometimes pejoratively referred to as "name it and claim it" theology, suggests that when believers speak or "declare" something in faith, they can actually bring it about in real life.[8]

8. Taylor, *Violent Take It by Force*, 32.

In this view, faith isn't just about trusting God; it's a spiritual force that gets activated by belief. Since God wants us to prosper, we can attain health, wealth, healing, and success by genuinely believing we will attain these in faith.[9] These ideas are supported by biblical passages like Mark 11:23–24, which says, "Truly I tell you, if you say to this mountain, 'Be taken up and thrown into the sea,' and if you do not doubt in your heart but believe that what you say will come to pass, it will be done for you. So I tell you, whatever you ask for in prayer, believe that you have received it, and it will be yours."

One major issue with Word of Faith theology is that it views faith as transactional: If you believe correctly and say the right things, then you can unlock something in the spiritual world. Although I'm sure most folks in the Word of Faith movement are believers who genuinely love God, there are some tough implications tied to this theology. A transactional view of faith gives a person power *over* God, which, when they attempt to bind spiritual forces to serve their own desires, seems jarringly like witchcraft. The Word of Faith movement redefines faith as a force that can be controlled, kind of like the Force in *Star Wars*. Instead of trusting God, we try to wield God's power. To steer clear of this, we should always view faith as trust in God's leading, not as a means to manipulate outcomes. We must bind our wills to God's, not God's to ours. While God desires to bless, heal, and provide for us, it might happen in ways we don't expect. Faith is trusting God even through those uncertainties.[10]

The Real Power of Naming

The *real* power of naming things is less about control and more about identity formation. According to linguist Eyo Mensah, parents tend to communicate their beliefs and expectations for their child through the act of naming. By naming, people gain "social capital which simultaneously reinforces community solidarity and

9. Kenneth Hagin's short book *Words* encapsulates this theology well. See Kenneth Hagin, *Words* (Faith Library, 1979).

10. This is a topic we'll flesh out in the next chapter.

cohesion."[11] In other words, naming helps situate both the child and the family into a socioreligious community. Names place people and give them contexts.

Names also influence how people see themselves and are perceived by others. For example, have you ever seen someone start to live into their own nickname? Back in college, I worked as a server at an Italian restaurant. One night, I gave one of my server buddies the nickname "Cap" because he kind of looked like Captain America. It caught on—soon after, most of the staff started calling him Cap, and, sure enough, he naturally stepped up as a leader for our team. It could have been his build and strong character that drove him to lead, or maybe it was because many of us were already referring to him as our captain. Either way, Cap lived into his named identity.

Nicknames can also make people feel included in a group. When I was a youth pastor, I used to give everyone nicknames. The names were often silly and meaningless (some of my top picks were "Winkle," "T Rey Rey," and "Cheat-O") but seemed to make the students feel valued. The members of our group weren't nameless faces when they entered the youth room but known students with full backstories. The nicknames often began as inside jokes from fleeting moments, but they ultimately created a sense of belonging. These students were part of our tribe.

Apparently, Jesus was a notorious nicknamer too. Peter's actual name was Simon, but Jesus calls him Peter, which means "the Rock" or "Rocky." When Jesus says, "And I tell you, you are Peter, and on this rock I will build my church, and the gates of Hades will not prevail against it" (Matt. 16:18), he is making a clever play on words. Jesus also calls James and John "the Sons of Thunder." Peter, James, and John are among Jesus's closest disciples—and, according to Christian tradition, they bravely and faithfully lead the church after Jesus's

11. Eyo Mensah, "The Appropriation of Animal Names as Personal Names in Ibibio and Tiv Onomastic Traditions in Nigeria: An Ethnopragmatic Study," in *Personal Names and Naming from an Anthropological-Linguistic Perspective*, ed. Sambulo Ndlovu (De Gruyter, 2023), 220.

ascension to heaven. Looks like Rocky and the Sons of Thunder lived into their named identities too!

With all this talk about the power of naming, the questions we must ask in our politically divisive age are: Who are we allowing to name us? What labels (or nicknames) are we embracing and living into? And are we being formed or malformed by what we are named?

Resisting Malforming Labels

Being a philosophical and artistic type, I've always hated labels. I find that artists live in a sort of paradox; they make work in order to express themselves and to be understood, but as soon as they start being understood they get uncomfortable and rebel against whatever it is anyone thinks of them. It's likely why artists like Picasso and Bob Dylan had so many eras throughout their careers. Dylan, in particular, always turned down the labels that others wanted to assign to him—be it folk artist, protest singer, poet, or any other category. This is evidenced by a 1966 interview with Paul Jay Robbins, where Dylan famously remarked, "All I can do is be me, whoever that is."[12] He viewed identity as something flexible and imaginative, not something set in stone.

I too have always rebelled against typecasting. I was a straight-A student who had long hair and was in a metal band. I'm Puerto Rican and German with a slight Southern drawl (and I hate sweet tea!). I was a pastor sporting tattoos. I used to say things—first subconsciously, but later on purpose—to challenge what people expected of me. I'd tell theologians that I'm a songwriter, musicians that I'm a visual artist, and so forth. Ironically, though, I've realized that rejecting other people's expectations of me is still a reaction to their expectations.[13] If I let what others think influence my decisions, even in opposition, aren't I still letting them determine my identity? I've learned to accept

12. Bob Dylan and Paul Jay Robbins, "Bob Dylan as Dylan," *Fifth Estate*, no. 11 (July 30, 1966), https://www.fifthestate.org/archive/11-july-30-1966/bob-dylan-as-dylan.

13. Moeller and D'Ambrosio, *You and Your Profile*, 172.

some labels (theologian, artist, Pentecostal) but still refuse to let any of these define me ultimately—not because I'm stubborn but because I've grown in the conviction that we must be selective of what people call us or put onto us. Because names and labels have formational power and we tend to live into them, we must scrutinize what we allow people to call us.

The Bible consistently encourages us to fully identify with and dedicate ourselves to God. In Isaiah, God reassures the Israelites, saying, "Do not fear, for I have redeemed you; I have called you by name; you are mine" (Isa. 43:1). Broadly applied, this passage suggests that when God redeems us, we are named and claimed by God. Furthermore, the Bible tells us that redemption transforms us into a new creation: "So if anyone is in Christ, there is a new creation: everything old has passed away; look, new things have come into being!" (2 Cor. 5:17). Our redemption through Christ should inspire our complete devotion to God: "It is no longer I who live, but it is Christ who lives in me. And the life I now live in the flesh I live by the faith of the Son of God, who loved me and gave himself for me" (Gal. 2:20). As our old self dies, we uncover our new life and identity in union with Jesus.

As mentioned in chapter 2, when Moses is given the first two commandments, Yahweh states, "You shall not bow down to them or serve them, for I the Lord your God am a jealous God" (Exod. 20:5). God isn't okay with sharing the throne with anyone or anything, and this means that we shouldn't identify with anyone or anything that opposes God. Actually, we must make our identity in God foundational for everything else. To do otherwise is to chase shadows, thinking that they are what's real. God's jealousy reminds us that the shadows only exist in reference to the light. In other words, everything exists because of God and is thus contingent on God, so what's *truly* real is God.

Chapter 2 discussed religious pluralism and how God does not have many names. Rather, God has a singular, covenantal name ("I am" or Yahweh) that God reveals to Moses in Exodus 3:14–15:

> God said to Moses, "I am who I am." He said further, "Thus you shall say to the Israelites, 'I am has sent me to you.'" God also said to

> Moses, "Thus you shall say to the Israelites, 'The Lord, the God of your ancestors, the God of Abraham, the God of Isaac, and the God of Jacob, has sent me to you':
>
> This is my name forever,
> and this my title for all generations."

Throughout the Old Testament, the Israelites are told to lift up and call on the name of Yahweh alone (Deut. 28:58; Ps. 83:18; Isa. 42:8; Mic. 4:5; Zech. 14:9; Mal. 1:11). In the New Testament, when Jesus is identified as the incarnation of Yahweh, we see that the name of Jesus is "the name that is above every other name" (Phil. 2:9), that "there is no other name under heaven given among mortals by which we must be saved" (Acts 4:12), and that "everyone who calls on the name of the Lord shall be saved" (Rom. 10:13). In Matthew's birth narrative of Jesus, Joseph is instructed to name the child Jesus, "for he will save his people from their sins" (Matt. 1:21). This is significant. The name we translate as "Jesus" in English comes from the Aramaic name Yeshua (יֵשׁוּעַ), a shortened form of the Hebrew *Yehoshua* (יְהוֹשֻׁעַ), which means "Yahweh is salvation." Jesus's name wasn't just a randomly chosen name—it reveals Christ's purpose to embody God's saving power. Through Jesus, Yahweh becomes personal and visible. Indeed, Yahweh *is* salvation, and it is by Yeshua, the incarnation of Yahweh, that we are saved.

Since God created us and Jesus saves us, we should not only feel okay being named and claimed by God, but we'll see that the name God gives us resonates more deeply than anything else we could ever imagine. The name God gives us rings true, cutting through the clutter of worldly labels and identities that are put on us. While Jesus's name means "Yahweh is salvation," your name, whatever it sounds like, means "beloved, child of God." You are the object of Christ's mission, his reason for the cross. You are Christ's beloved. This is the true label and name that you and I must live into.

The name God gives us is both a personal and a family name. A **family name** (a surname or last name) is the part of a name that shows which family or lineage a person comes from. Our name indicates that we are part of God's family. Most social theorists say that humans are tribal by nature,[14] and the Bible seems to agree. The Bible says we're in covenant either with God or with our flesh (Rom. 5:13–19); we're a citizen of God's kingdom or of the kingdom of the world (Col. 1:13–14); we're in God's family or are children of the devil (1 John 3). We can't live into both realities; we must choose one.

This point can help us understand the meaning of 666 in the book of Revelation. The mark of the beast is not a tattoo, vaccine, or computer chip implanted into our foreheads. It is a label. Revelation 13:18 says, "This calls for wisdom: let anyone with understanding calculate the number of the beast, for it is the number for a person. Its number is six hundred sixty-six." Notice that this passage says it's "the number of a person," not just some random code. Many scholars think it refers to Caesar Nero, using **gematria**—a Hebrew alphanumeric system where every letter has a specific numerical value.[15] You can write out a name in Hebrew and then add up the values of its letters to arrive at a number. Early readers, who were familiar with gematria, would probably have tried to decode it using Hebrew letters. The Latin name "Neron Caesar" looks like this when transliterated into Hebrew letters: נרון קסר,or NRWN QSR. When you add up the numerical values of these letters, they total 666.[16] Hence, the mark of the beast represents total allegiance to Rome's leader, Nero.

In Revelation, people are made to put the mark of the beast on their foreheads or their right hands in order to buy or sell anything (13:16–17). This means they have to label themselves and align

14. See Samuel Bowels and Herbert Gintis, *A Cooperative Species: Human Reciprocity and Its Evolution* (Princeton University Press, 2013), 48; Edward Wilson, *On Human Nature* (Harvard University Press, 2012), 157; Avi Tuschman, *Our Political Nature: The Evolutionary Origins of What Divides Us* (Prometheus Books, 2013), 22.

15. See N. T. Wright, *Revelation for Everyone*, 20th anniv. ed. (Westminster John Knox, 2023), 90; Michael Gorman, *Reading Revelation Responsibly: Uncivil Worship and Witness; Following the Lamb into the New Creation* (Cascade Books, 2011), 126; G. K. Beale with David Campbell, *Revelation: A Shorter Commentary* (Eerdmans, 2015), 284–85.

16. Some early manuscripts of Revelation actually say 616 instead of 666. This is because in Latin, if you drop the last *n* in "Neron," Nero Caesar equals 616 in gematria.

themselves with Rome or be excluded from normal life and cut off from society. But the mark isn't only practical—it symbolizes a spiritual and political allegiance to Nero, who was the figurehead of Rome, a godless empire that opposed God's kingdom. N. T. Wright points out that the number 666 is also a parody of the number of perfection, 777, or possibly even 888, which, using gematria, comes out to JESUS.[17]

A lot of people miss, however, that in Revelation, God's people are also marked on their foreheads. The very next chapter after the 666 passage says the 144,000, representing God's chosen people, "had his name and his Father's name written on their foreheads" (14:1). And at the end of Revelation, John describes the New Jerusalem by writing, "Nothing accursed will be found there any more. But the throne of God and of the Lamb will be in it, and his servants will worship him; they will see his face, and his name will be on their foreheads" (22:3–4). All this is to say, there's no spiritual neutrality in Revelation. There's no Switzerland; we must choose a side. Christ's redemption and reign isn't only about the defeat of sin. It signals in us a complete transformation—a shift in identity, allegiance, and covenantal relationship. We're always in a tribe, but are we part of God's tribe or someone else's? Whose name is written on your forehead?

Identity Malformation and Political Reductionisms

We've taken quite the scenic route to get to this chapter's destination. While this chapter is about hearing God through the noise of coercive politics, I felt it was important to slow down and clarify how naming and power are depicted in the Bible. This is essential, as it shapes how Christians should approach political allegiance and identity formation. In these divisive political times, the left and right continually try to enlist us into an ideological turf war. We're prodded to pick sides, wear political labels, and sell out to the causes of politicians and their stakeholders. At first, we might be passive observers, but

17. Wright, *Revelation for Everyone*, 90.

before long, we too find ourselves demeaning others, mistrusting one another, name-calling, and causing all sorts of trouble, all while feeding into the anger and fear that's stoked by either political party. Today, we see neighbors, friends, coworkers, and family members pitted against each other just to back the next leaders of our nation—and we're accomplices.

A Clash of Identities

This political season is so divisive because we're seeing a clash of identities. Instead of only allowing God to foundationally name and define us, many Christians in the West want God *and* their political party to define them and shape their identities. Naming is at the root of this issue. People may not say this outright, but their syncretic actions prove otherwise. Remember, however, that God is a jealous God, so a "God and country" identity just won't work. But given that we *do* exist in a political reality, what should a Christian's relationship to a nation look like?

In my book *The Problem and Promise of Freedom*, I argue that Christians must view their political allegiance differently than their allegiance to the kingdom of God. In God's kingdom, every believer willingly enters into a covenant with God. Since the creator of everything is the Lord of the covenant, a covenant with God is all-encompassing and shapes every part of our lives. As covenant partners, Christians depend entirely on God, who's the provider, and interact with one another, the stewards, in God's kingdom. Those who are in covenant with God have a duty to serve, trust, and be accountable to God and God's people.[18]

A political state, in contrast, requires a commitment to a **social contract**—a deal between a people and their government to create a society where all agree to follow certain rules, rights, and responsibilities for every citizen's benefit. To govern our society, the state requires us to follow the rule of law. Yet, as citizens, we yearn to maintain as much freedom as we can while submitting to the minimal

18. Félix-Jäger, *Problem and Promise of Freedom*, 90–91.

number of obligatory rules established for the common good. This sort of arrangement is very different from a covenant. Covenants are all-consuming, while contracts are binding but limited in scope, only determining the terms of a particular agreement. Given this distinction, we should say that Christians relate to a nation as contracted citizens but dwell in the kingdom of God as covenant partners.[19]

It's important to keep this distinction in mind, since we're more prone to finding our identities in a covenant than in a contract. For example, your identity will definitely be shaped by a marriage covenant, but let's hope it isn't as deeply affected by the terms and conditions of an iPhone contract. That's not to say we aren't shaped by mundane things like phone carriers—everything shapes us to some degree. But the formative scope of a covenant is much greater than that of a contract. We want our identity to be foundationally formed by Christ in God's kingdom and then derivatively formed everywhere else. Hence, we must remember that our relationship to a nation resides within a social contract.

I would argue, however, that nations frequently overstep and attempt to require from us the sort of allegiance congruent with a covenant, not a contract. Not only do they ask us to live in a society as good citizens; they ask us to pledge allegiance to a nation as a covenant partner. We're socialized and asked to "perform" our loyalty in order to maintain our public identity as good national citizens.

I want to be clear: National pride is not the issue. You should see me when the Olympics come around. I've never been prouder to be an American than when I watched Lebron James and Steph Curry join forces to whoop France on their home turf during the 2024 Olympics! We can definitely be proud of our nations, upbringings, and cultures.

Nor is it a problem that *some* of our identity is shaped by our nation. We are all inevitably shaped, to some degree, by where we live and how we function in a society. I can't help but think like an American wherever I am, since the US is where I was brought up and socialized.

19. Félix-Jäger, *Problem and Promise of Freedom*, 101–2.

The problem is when the nation inserts itself as a primary source for identity formation—when the nation creeps up on Christ's throne and wants to shape our identity equally with Christ. The problem is when our national identity takes on a religious fervor—one that's totalizing and all-consuming. We know that our covenantal relationship with God means that Christ is the Lord of every aspect of our lives. But when a nation demands that we regard our citizenship with that same intensity, it's essentially asking us to idolize it, to see it as our co-lord with Christ.

Some people confuse being a disciple of Christ with advancing a political party's ideology. God does not endorse a political party, nor is God for one worldly nation over another. In Matthew 28:18–20, Jesus says, "All authority in heaven and on earth has been given to me. Go therefore and make disciples of all nations, baptizing them in the name of the Father and of the Son and of the Holy Spirit and teaching them to obey everything that I have commanded you. And remember, I am with you always, to the end of the age." Jesus calls his disciples to make disciples of all nations, *not* to make Christian nations. Christ being Lord over every sector of our lives does not mean we should force our Christian ideals onto a polis. Jesus himself did not do this in Israel or in Rome. Jesus never commissioned us to form a Christian political party but to go make disciples. His kingdom is not of this world (John 18:36), and he couldn't care less what nation his children are brought up in. He cares that his children know him.

In the US, we are pushed to align ourselves with a political party and told that, somehow, identification with that party and its political leaders is a Christian action. But this is far from the heart of Christ. In reality, we're manipulated by the world's political forces to embrace an ideology with totalizing fervor. When we're radicalized toward the right or left, we begin to easily demonize others and thwart any possibility of genuine discourse. And if politics makes it so we can't even talk to each other, then how can we possibly share the love of Christ with one another? In a world where we're pushed to make political enemies and to view people through the lens of red or blue, Christ calls us to look at people through the lens of blood and water—the redness of his blood and the blueness of his water that flowed from his side, down the cross, and onto all the iniquities we left at its foot. The cross enables us to reconcile with God and each other.

The Problem of Political Buzzwords

In their book *The Myth of Left and Right*, political scientists and brothers Hyrum and Verlan Lewis claim that there's no single "essence" that comprises the views of a leftist or liberal ideology, nor is there a single root that connects a rightist or conservative ideology.[20] They argue that the left-right spectrum in American politics isn't set in stone or even ideologically coherent, since there's no stable set of principles that clearly defines what "left" or "right" means over time. For instance, President Theodore Roosevelt, a Republican, championed environmental conservation, but environmentalism is now viewed as a progressive cause.[21] There's presently a conservative swing toward isolationism, but both Presidents Eisenhower and Reagan supported international alliances and global free trade.[22] Both left and right ideologies have sought to regulate various moral issues at different times (e.g., sanctioning prohibition, regulating harmful speech, or mandating diversity efforts). What is considered left-wing or right-wing changes throughout history and can often be contradictory.

There's also variety within these big-tent ideologies. Within conservatism today, there's a pull toward both deficit spending and balancing budgets.[23] There's variance between support for global free markets and "America first" protectionism, and on whether conservatives should support limited governments or have expansive military budgets. Within liberalism, there's a pull for personal choice on some moral issues (e.g., abortion or gender identity) and for government

20. Hyrum Lewis and Verlan Lewis, *The Myth of Left and Right: How the Political Spectrum Misleads and Harms America* (Oxford University Press, 2023), 5.

21. Lewis and Lewis, *Myth of Left and Right*, 11.

22. Lewis and Lewis, *Myth of Left and Right*, 73.

23. Deficit spending seemed to be one of the major causes for the fallout between Trump and Musk over 2025's so-called Big Beautiful Bill.

mandates on others (e.g., public health or hate speech). Some on the left want to work against corporate greed, while others want to support and incentivize multibillion-dollar tech industries. It is difficult to find consistent conservative or liberal principles even within party lines.

Moreover, it's not possible for people to completely fit into a left or right ideology. Because these ideologies are stitched together and not consistent, a person can hold a conservative idea that contradicts another conservative idea. And if you ask people about specific issues, they'll probably find themselves unintentionally identifying with both parties.

Hyrum Lewis and Verlan Lewis share an example of how this spectrum fails by using teenager stereotypes: "There are two types of teenagers in America: Jocks and Nerds. Jocks are athletic, dumb, and attractive while Nerds are clumsy, smart, and ugly. Those of moderate looks, athleticism, and intelligence fall in the middle between the Jock-Nerd extremes. All high school students and groups can be placed somewhere on this 'teenage spectrum.'"[24] Yet we can all think of young people who embody traits from both ends of the spectrum, like smart athletes and those who are both good-looking and a bit clumsy. In the same way, an American could be opposed to corporate greed and support racial justice (left), while also being pro-life and advocating for school choice (right). In fact, a lot of Christians hold these mixed views on political issues. So do Americans really subscribe wholesale to essentialist political ideologies? Is it even possible to do so?

The Lewises argue that what we see in the US is not allegiance to various ideologies but tribal support for a party. Defined as the way individuals see themselves, others, and the world, where the main reference point is a group,[25] **tribalism** is our natural tendency

24. Lewis and Lewis, *Myth of Left and Right*, 13.

25. Nikos Sotirakopoulos, *Identity Politics and Tribalism: The New Culture Wars* (Societas, 2021), 18. Sotirakopoulos argues that we can combat tribalism by fostering a belief in individual agency (190). I don't agree. I believe that humans are inescapably tribal (or covenantal, to use a theological term) by nature. Rather than thinking we

to create exclusive groups and then prioritize loyalty and the group's interests over those of others. The Lewises argue that it's a tribal partisan identity that shapes ideology, not the reverse.[26] In other words, people often adjust their views to fit their political group instead of selecting a group that matches their essential beliefs. They form their opinions based on party allegiance rather than on strong ideological beliefs. The left-right spectrum thus promotes political tribalism by establishing a false dichotomy. You must be all-in on one specific view of the ideology (likely the view of those in political power), or you're labeled as inauthentic and not a true member of the tribe.[27] This tribal mentality suppresses independent thought, as people feel compelled to align with whatever their side currently supports, even if it goes against previous positions. To foreground that the left and right don't exist as coherent ideologies, I'll refer to them as the "tribal right" and the "tribal left."

Tribal partisan identities promote reduced versions of reality. Pundits and politicians simplify things to a few principles and then convince us that they are consistent with the entire ideology. They vilify the opposing party and lead us to believe that the political divide is actually a battle of good versus evil. Tribal loyalty results in unquestioning acceptance of whatever the party decides. Because of tribal loyalty, Christians are pressured to morally defend their party's actions, even when those actions contradict a biblical worldview.

By using political buzzwords, pundits and politicians reinforce a politically tribal identity by reducing and branding the other side. Both sides have employed name-calling to caricature the opposition so it can be easily criticized. Members of the tribal left call members of the tribal right "fascists," "bigots," and "white supremacists." Because of their policies and rhetoric, the tribal right is often accused of being gun-toting misogynists, science deniers, intolerant homophobes, nationalists, and conspiracy theorists. Similarly, the

---

can exist as individuals outside of a tribe, our task is to make sure we align with the right tribe, which I argue is the kingdom of God.

26. Lewis and Lewis, *Myth of Left and Right*, 72.

27. Lewis and Lewis, *Myth of Left and Right*, 39.

tribal right has called the tribal left "communists," "snowflakes," and "globalists," and lumped together support for DEI (diversity, equity, and inclusion), critical race theory, gender inclusivity, feminism, climate justice, and LGBTQ+ rights as being "woke."

The word "woke" has its roots in Black slang from almost a century ago. "Staying woke" meant being informed and aware about social injustices and racial disparities.[28] The word has since been rebranded as a political buzzword. **Wokeness** is now a controversial and politicized term that basically refers to progressive worldviews that oppose systemic injustices and support identity politics and social activism. Like other political buzzwords, wokeness can mean many things, and it's always reductive. There are several waves of feminism, but feminists in general are called woke. There are many ways to support climate justice, but environmentalists in general are called woke. There are many ways to support racial justice, but the general promotion of diversity is called woke. This name-calling gets so extreme that even being empathetic toward others is called woke.[29] What good is it to call anything woke when there are no legitimate criteria for what is constituted as being woke? It's an ambiguous pejorative used to categorize anything that tribal right ideologues despise and to reduce and discard ideas and people. On the contrary, we're called to be ministers of reconciliation—to break down walls between people, not to raise new walls by demonizing people through pejoratives.

One of the main vehicles for political tribalism has been **identity politics**, a way of engaging politics so that people focus on issues that are significant to their particular social groups, such as race, gender, sexuality, or nationality. Typically, on the tribal left, identity politics emerge as a response to persistent marginalization. For instance,

28. Kiara Alfonseca, "What Does 'Woke' Mean and Why Are Some Conservatives Using It?," ABC News, March 4, 2025, https://abcnews.go.com/Politics/woke-conservatives/story?id=93051138.

29. Tiffany Stanley, "Is Empathy a Sin? Some Conservative Christians Argue It Can Be," PBS News, August 21, 2025, https://www.pbs.org/newshour/politics/is-empathy-a-sin-some-conservative-christians-argue-it-can-be.

movements like #MeToo, Black Lives Matter, and Pride Month celebrations are all recent and ongoing expressions of identity politics in the US, often bringing attention to and politicizing certain facets of a person's identity to advance social causes associated with that identity. The tribal right also engages in identity politics, but in its own way. For instance, white nationalists who seek to preserve white culture in the US, such as by framing affirmative action as "reverse racism," can also be viewed as engaging in identity politics that are rooted in matters of race and culture.[30] This clash of tribal identities has formed the latest iteration of America's culture wars, which continue to bring about deep division and polarization.

Through political tribalism and name-calling, we can see a trend emerge: Complex identities or beliefs are reduced to a single label that's easy to criticize, ridicule, or cancel. The tribal right uses name-calling to "own the libs," and the tribal left uses social pressure to "cancel" dissenting voices. Although these are the terms often associated with each tribe, both tribes try to "own" or "cancel" each other in their own ways. When labels are thrown around carelessly or too broadly, they can shut down dialogue, spread hate, and encourage deeper political tribalism. Not only do we hurt others by reducing them to a label, but we hurt ourselves when we identify and begin to live into the labels that are put on us.

The Lewises suggest that we move away from this basic left-right model and instead "go granular," focusing on issue-specific conversations. Instead of aligning ourselves with an overarching political identity, we should name specific things we support. Instead of saying someone is right-wing, we should say they are "against free trade." Instead of calling someone a jock, we should say they're "on the tennis team."[31] Being specific not only makes our language more precise; it also helps us avoid the baggage that accompanies reductionism. This suggestion is also helpful because it aids us in keeping our distance from political tribalism. It allows us to resist labels while still

30. Sotirakopoulos, *Identity Politics and Tribalism*, 25.
31. Lewis and Lewis, *Myth of Left and Right*, 89.

advocating for what we believe in and gives us the courage and clarity to criticize our own leaders when we believe they are governing against God's will.

While this is good advice for political clarity, I'd like to argue in the rest of this chapter that the best way to leave a bad tribe is to be grafted into a better one. To evade political tribalism, we must properly align ourselves with God's tribe—the only tribe that should be foundationally identity-forming in the first place.

Worship and Identity Formation

As we talk about hearing God and following the Spirit through politically tenuous times, the first and most obvious thing we must discern is which tribe we belong to. We must ask where our allegiance truly lies: Are we national citizens or kingdom people first? Which tribe is shaping our values, and which vision of the future is driving our current actions? What takes priority for us—our racial, sexual, or national identities, or our identity as beloved children of God? Who is labeling us? Whose name is written on our foreheads? We shouldn't rush to answer these questions or we might end up only saying what we know *should* be true. We must respond to these questions vulnerably to uncover what is true in our lives as proven by our actions. This is where discernment can be painful. If we've given away something of ourselves—something that belongs to God—to a political tribe, it's time to repent.

You might think this sounds a bit extreme. Surely it's possible to strike a balance between living as Christians and as worldly citizens? Isn't moderation a good thing? In most situations, yes; but in this instance, I'd argue that it's not. We need to somberly consider what it means to call Jesus our Lord. We have to take seriously what the Bible says about God being a jealous God. It's precisely our instinct for balance, applied to God, that the Bible warns us against. God's lordship can never be divided. Any part of the created order, which includes our racial, gender, or national identities, cannot be above or on equal footing with God. God is infinite, and everything else is not. God is what's real, and everything else is derivative. This is one of those cases where an exclusive either/or disjunction is absolutely necessary and not a false dilemma or dichotomy. Jesus said, after all, "Whoever is not with me is against me, and whoever does not gather with me scatters" (Matt. 12:30). When it comes to lordship, moderation doesn't make sense either logically or biblically.

Realigning Through Worship

If we're going to be all-in with God, the first vital steps we must take are to recognize that we've been shaped by a worldly vision of life and then to repent. **Repentance** is a good thing. It means turning away from anything that's keeping us from God and turning toward God. This is how we realign with Christ and reaffirm his proper lordship. But how do we maintain a right alignment after repentance? How can we be so deeply formed into God's story that we're able to recognize when a politicized voice is trying to lead us astray? Simply, by worshiping God. That seems basic, but I'd argue that a major upshot of worship is being able to regularly align and realign with God's will, to continually make God's story ours.

Worship is a spiritual discipline that helps us conform our hearts, minds, wills, and desires to God's. Alongside prayer and Scripture reading, worship reinforces the Christian story, but it does so affectively and through repetition. Worship helps us to feel the story we embody—to know it deeply and emotionally, not just cognitively.

I've written extensively about the formational power of worship elsewhere,[32] but here I would like to focus on how worship shapes our identities in Christ and how worship can, therefore, be our best foil against political tribalism. According to Pentecostal theologian Frank Macchia, worship is where Christian identity is truly formed.[33] In worship we respond to God and to each other in light of what God

32. See Steven Félix-Jäger, *How to Worship for All Its Worth: A Guide for Pastors, Worship Leaders, and Students* (Zondervan Academic, 2025); and Steven Félix-Jäger, *Renewal Worship: A Theology of Pentecostal Doxology* (IVP Academic, 2022).

33. Frank Macchia, "Signs of Grace: Towards a Charismatic Theology of Worship," in *Toward a Pentecostal Theology of Worship*, ed. Lee Roy Martin (CPT, 2016), 154.

is doing in and through us. As we sway, lift our hands, and sing the same words together, we are communally molded and trained, able to unite in solidarity for spiritual formation. The kinds of Christians we aim to be are rehearsed through our patterns of worship that are centered by Scripture and that direct our actions.[34] Theologian David Lemley writes that through worship, "a new identity is possible and perhaps embraced, which emerges in the days between Sundays. Worship shapes a way of life, and the concrete lives of worshipers."[35] We learn and grow together in worship, which, as Macchia notes, "brings right belief into life so that it might then nourish and support life witness. Worship is the context in which the church lives the biblical story in resistance to the world and in witness to an alternative reality."[36]

Think about the identity-forming words we sing in worship every week. We often sing about the lordship of Christ and the exclusivity of his name. For example, the pre-chorus of Chris Tomlin's song "Holy Forever" demonstrates how the name of Jesus exceeds every political reality:

> All thrones and dominions, all powers and positions
> Your name stands above them all[37]

Similarly, just before stating that Jesus's name is above all other names, the bridge of Hillsong Worship's "What a Beautiful Name" says,

> You have no rival, You have no equal
> Now and forever, God You reign[38]

34. David Lemley, *Becoming What We Sing: Formation Through Contemporary Worship Music* (Eerdmans, 2021), 7.

35. Lemley, *Becoming What We Sing*, 28.

36. Macchia, "Signs of Grace," 154.

37. "Holy Forever," words and music by Brian Johnson, Chris Tomlin, Jason Ingram, Jenn Johnson, Phil Wickham, CCLI #7201044 © 2022 Brian and Jenn Publishing; Capitol CMG Paragon; S. D. G. Publishing, Be Essential Songs; My Magnolia Music; Phil Wickham Music; Simply Global Songs; Bethel Music Publishing (administrated by Bethel Music Publishing, Capitol CMG Publishing, Essential Music Publishing LLC).

38. "What a Beautiful Name," words and music by Ben Fielding and Brooke Ligertwood, CCLI #7068424 © 2016 Hillsong Music Publishing Australia (administrated by Hillsong Music Publishing).

Both songs highlight the name of God and reaffirm Christ's lordship. Even though these songs were written by evangelical and Pentecostal worship leaders, they carry a broad theological message and are sung all over the world and across various denominations and traditions.

We also sing songs that talk about our personal identities in Christ. For instance, Hillsong Worship's "Who You Say I Am" talks about embracing the identity that Christ gives us (and about belonging in "a place for me" in the Father's house). The bridge repeats these lines:

> I am chosen, not forsaken
> I am who You say I am[39]

Similarly, Bethel Music's "No Longer Slaves" states that being a child of God makes us no longer a slave of fear. To establish the theme of adoption, the second verse says,

> I've been born again to your family
> Your blood flows through my veins[40]

There are many more songs that share themes of naming and identity formation, but I wanted to highlight just a few from my own tradition that have become fairly ubiquitous in contemporary worship. Every denomination and tradition has similar songs about identity formation, and it's crucial that we sing them. When we sing about who we are in Christ—beloved, redeemed, chosen, and forgiven—we're expressing the most foundational truths about ourselves that no earthly label can obscure. As we sing those words to God, we also proclaim those identity-forming words over ourselves.

39. "Who You Say I Am," words and music by Brooke Ligertwood and Reuben Morgan, CCLI #7102401 © 2017 Hillsong Music Publishing Australia (administrated by Hillsong Music Publishing USA).

40. "No Longer Slaves," words and music by Brian Johnson, Joel Case, Jonathan David Helser, CCLI #7030123 © 2014 Quiltmaker Music; Bethel Music Publishing (administrated by Bethel Music Publishing).

Home Is Where We Worship Together

Since we live in an earthly society but our real citizenship is in God's kingdom, Stanley Hauerwas and William Willimon refer to us not as citizens but as "resident aliens" in this world.[41] Because the church is made up of such people, we must steer clear of being politically domesticated by the world. In worship, we're reminded again and again of our true citizenship. In worship, we come together as members of a kingdom that's not of this world. We gain a cosmic vision, seeing the world through the lens of our eternal redemption. We learn to live rightly when our identities are formed as kingdom people, recognizing once again that the world isn't our home; it's our mission field.

As a biracial person, I've never felt completely at home anywhere. My vision of the world and my first memories were formed in Germany, so I primarily see the world visually, the way Germans do. But my closest sense of kinship is with my Puerto Rican family, with whom I feel most loved and known. I've lived the majority of my life in the US, and several cities feel nostalgic to me. But none of the places I've lived have ever truly felt like home. Someone who's grown up in one place might have a deeper sense of what belonging to a specific locale feels like, but my mixed identity has shown me that we feel at home with people, not in places.

I've traveled to different countries and experienced various cultures, attending many different worship services along the way. Every time, everywhere I've gone, I've felt most at home among Christians who love and worship Jesus. In worship, I hear the name of Jesus being lifted up. I see hands raised high. I feel that same Spirit moving through the foreign (to me) congregation. Even if I don't understand every word, I somehow understand everything that's important. In those moments, I'm not just an American or a Puerto Rican or a German or a visitor to whatever place I am in. I'm not an outsider or

41. Stanley Hauerwas and William Willimon, *Resident Aliens: A Provocative Christian Assessment of Culture and Ministry for People Who Know That Something Is Wrong* (Abingdon, 1989), 24.

a stranger. I am *home*. The people I worship with are family because we're united by the one who transcends every one of our worldly differences. Whenever I join in worship with fellow believers around the world, I remember that our real identities aren't defined by where we come from but by who we belong to.

The world believes that belonging is somehow decided by borders, pledges, and anthems. But kingdom citizenship says belonging is not expressed through a pledge but proclaimed through a doxology, one that resonates globally. In fact, feeling at home with the global church is a clear sign of God's kingdom. It's a preview of the time when people from "every nation, from all tribes and peoples and languages, standing before the throne and before the Lamb, robed in white, with palm branches in their hands," worship the Lord in unity (Rev. 7:9). In a world divided by nationalisms, tribalisms, and political idols, the church should be a unique and beautiful community that speaks various languages but worships the same Lord, residing in different nations but bending the knee to the same king, the king of kings.

When we sing about being God's sons and daughters, we would do well to recognize that God's household extends far beyond our national borders. Worship songs that focus on our identity encourage us to look up and recognize that every believer in the world is part of the same body (1 Cor. 12:12–27). Worship that is beautiful and true acknowledges and even celebrates differences, placing us in a larger story where the cross has already broken down every dividing wall. We can't let politics get in the way of what the Spirit is doing in our lives and in the world around us. If we're ever feeling the pressure of coercive politics, one of the best things we can do is get together with our family of faith and worship our Lord.[42]

42. Without spending too much time here, I want to say that I find the worship protests that were going on in the US during the COVID-19 pandemic to be problematic. Although many people desired to worship Jesus, much of what was going on seemed like political propaganda. What often emerged was a mixed, syncretized message of faith and politics. One of the main points of this chapter is that nothing should share the throne with Christ, and these worship protests seemed to give equal footing to Christ and a particular political party.

Conclusion

This political season will pass. Governments come and go. Leaders change. Movements rise and fade away. History shows us that many once-powerful empires and ideologies now only exist in textbooks. Even still, we tend to get caught up in politics, mixing God's values with our nation's. When we uncritically fixate on a political vision, we're inevitably led to feelings of fear, anger, tribalism, or idolatry—our political allegiance turns into a spiritual identity. But when we acknowledge the temporariness of any political era, we're more apt to see things clearly and dissociate the things of this world from the things of God. We're better able to participate in civic life without being consumed by it.

This chapter argued that worship is one powerful way to steer clear from the seductions of power and politics and to focus on God's voice and the Spirit's leading. Worship helps us recalibrate our relationships with God and others and inspires our witness of Christ to the world. Because we're formed holistically in worship, it becomes a great foil against the spiritual malformations that come about through political tribalism. In this chapter, we've learned that words have power. Names have power. In worship, we recite God's holy name and remember the names God has given us. When we center our lives on Christ through worship, we remember who we are—and no political tribe can compete with that. While this chapter focused on staying the course and following the Spirit past the pull of political tribalism, the next chapter will discuss what it means to follow the Spirit in the midst of crisis when it's hard to discern where God is leading.

KEY WORDS

- **dominion theology**: A theological viewpoint that asserts Christians should have authority or dominion over every sector of life, including government, culture, law, and society

- **family name**: The part of a name that shows which family or lineage a person comes from
- **gematria**: A Hebrew alphanumeric system where every letter has a specific numerical value
- **identity**: The way people and groups perceive and convey who they are in relation to social roles, relationships, and norms
- **identity politics**: A way of engaging politics where people focus on issues that are significant to their particular social groups, such as race, gender, sexuality, or nationality
- **kingdom of God**: The reality where Christ is king and the whole world is at shalom
- **repentance**: Turning away from anything that's keeping us from God and turning toward God
- **shalom**: A life of peace, completeness, and holistic well-being
- **social contract**: A deal between a people and a government to create a society where all agree to follow certain rules, rights, and responsibilities for everyone's benefit
- **tribalism**: The way individuals see themselves, others, and the world, where the main reference point is the group
- **wokeness**: A pejorative describing progressive worldviews that oppose systemic injustices and that support identity politics and social activism

DISCUSSION QUESTIONS

- How formational have politics been for your identity? Have politics hurt your spiritual formation?
- Have you or someone you know ever faced accusations of being a "woke liberal" or a "conservative bigot"? How were those situations handled?
- Has worship ever sparked a reconciliation between you and someone else?

REFLECTION EXERCISE

Write a prayer for someone you disagree with politically. Be specific. Then, later in the week, serve or bless someone outside your political tribe, either in word or in deed.

five

Following the Spirit When It's Dark

I did everything right—or so I thought.

By the time I hit my early 30s, I held two master's degrees and a PhD in theology, had a few publications, and had gained quite a bit of experience as a high school teacher and an adjunct professor at various institutions. Teaching was my passion; I wanted to influence young minds and believed that God would use me to inspire the next generation to love and think deeply about God, the church, and the arts. I wanted to teach in higher ed, but after a string of unsuccessful job interviews in Florida, it seemed like those doors were completely shut.

Then one night, I saw a job posting in my inbox: "Private Christian high school in Southern California looking for a full-time art teacher." The position was similar to the teaching job I already held in Florida, but for my wife, Connie, and me, it felt like God was opening a door. It felt like a new beginning. After a flurry of Zoom interviews, I received the job offer.

That summer, Connie and I sold most of our stuff, packed up what was left, and loaded our whole lives into a U-Haul. Mila was just two years old then and too little to grasp the magnitude of the move, but she was all for the adventure, happily chattering from the back seat as we drove along the southern US border. After five days of road-tripping, we arrived at the Golden Coast.

For the first few months, everything was great. I enjoyed the students and quickly made friends with my new colleagues. The leadership was a bit disorganized but seemed clear about their goals. By January, however, cracks began to appear.

Payroll was late on multiple occasions. Leadership made promises, then walked them back. Rumors began circulating that the school's owner was mismanaging funds, and by April, it was clear that it wasn't just gossip. Suddenly the owner was MIA, and many of us began working unpaid in good faith. As the school year wrapped up, the harsh reality hit: The school was bankrupt. No one would receive their paychecks from April to June. There would be no severance. The whole staff and faculty submitted wage claims to the labor board, but we had already been unpaid for a couple months, and if there was going to be any resolution, it would take several more months for anything to materialize.

As can be expected, we were *really* struggling financially back then. Connie and I had sold almost everything just to make it to California, and now all our savings were wiped out, our credit cards were maxed, and we were barely scraping by with Connie's part-time job. We were completely lost as to what to do next. I had brought my wife and our little daughter across the country, but for what? I developed chest pains, acid reflux, and insomnia from the anxiety. For the first time in my adult life, I felt real shame. I had thought this opportunity would turn into something great. Instead, I felt like a failure.

Happily, that's not where the story ends, but we'll get to that later. I wanted to tell this story to frame the topic of our final chapter: following the Spirit when it's dark. Being a Christian does not mean we're exempt from trials and tribulations. In fact, the Bible says the opposite—it promises that we will experience trials and tribulations, and sometimes on account of Christ (Matt. 5:10–12; John 15:18–20). But while suffering is part of the Christian life, the Bible also promises that God will be with us (Heb. 4:15–16), that our faith produces perseverance (James 1:2–4), and that through our perseverance we'll grow in hope (Rom. 5:3–5). So while this chapter doesn't pretend to cure us of our suffering, it does offer guidance on what it means to follow the Spirit when God seems silent and when **anxiety**—a future-oriented, unrestrained worry[1]—starts to grab hold of us. Building off the last chapter, I'll argue that worship can build up our resilience and create in us the space to heal. As the opening story demonstrates, sometimes bad things happen to us, even when we've done everything right. In light of this, we'll kick this chapter off with the question "Where's God in all of this?"

Where's God?

Though Genesis is the first book in the Bible, many scholars think Job was actually written first. Job's story takes place in the land of Uz (Job 1:1) in Edom (Lam. 4:21), which is east of what would later become Israel. Can you guess the topic of the first book written in the Bible? The problem of suffering. I don't think that's a coincidence.

Job demonstrates how the world is full of injustice and pointless suffering. The book shows that even good people can endure hardships, and that God's reasons for what's happening are often hidden from us. Job, along with all the wisdom writers of the Bible, addresses these heavy themes head on. The writers cry out to God and colorfully express their struggles. Their pleas don't lead to easy, standard solutions to their problems. In fact, sometimes they don't find any solutions at all. Their solution is, at times, to trust God despite not having an answer.

After Job spends many chapters pleading with God and defending his innocence to his friends and neighbors, he finally manages to say,

> Though He slay me,
> I will hope in Him.
> Nevertheless I will argue my ways before Him. (Job 13:15 NASB)

1. J. Michael Jordan, *Worship in an Age of Anxiety: How Churches Can Create Space for Healing* (IVP Academic, 2024), 12.

Job refuses to be gaslit into thinking he did something wrong to deserve his suffering, yet he is able to reach a point of acceptance regarding his situation. Somehow, Job's willingness to confront his pain, name it, and fully engage with God during his suffering is enough of an answer for him.[2]

Job talks to God about everything. His relationship with God is raw, honest, and deeply personal. He questions God (10:3) and shows grief in its purest form. At one point, he even asks God, "Why did I not die at birth, come forth from the womb and expire?" (3:11). Even though Job has doubts, gets angry, and weeps, he keeps talking to God. Sometimes his prayers are confrontational and filled with rage, but they are still prayers. And that, I think, is the point. Job finds peace by sticking with God through his hardships. We have a lot to learn from Job here, which is evident by the many, many excellent books written about Job.[3] But when we consider Job, even if briefly, we might wonder how such an unjust world—one where a righteous man like Job could suffer so tremendously—is even possible, if God is good and all-powerful.

Suffering and the Consequences of Free Will

The **problem of evil**, sometimes called the problem of suffering, is one of the best-known philosophical challenges against the existence of God. The problem is not just an abstract debate—it's profoundly existential. People ask this question not only in philosophy classes but in hospital rooms, after tragedies, and during personal faith crises. It's the question Job asks when everything goes wrong in his life.

2. We know that Job's fortunes were restored by the end of the story, but can we really call that a true restoration? Job lost loved ones; new family members can't fill that void no matter how wonderful they are. But Job's restoration is actually beside the point. His resolve to trust God came *before* any restoration took place.

3. See John Walton and Tremper Longman III, *How to Read Job* (IVP, 2015); Christopher Ash, *Trusting God in the Darkness: A Guide to Understanding the Book of Job* (Crossway, 2021); Katharine Dell and Will Kynes, eds., *Reading Job Intertextually* (Bloomsbury, 2013); Richard Belcher Jr., *Job: The Mystery of Suffering and God's Sovereignty* (Christian Focus, 2017); and Francis Andersen, *Job: An Introduction and Commentary* (IVP Academic, 2008).

In its basic form, the problem of evil questions that God exists and can be both all-powerful and all-good. If that was so, then wouldn't God choose to stop evil? But since experiential evidence supports the existence of evil, the other three claims (God is all-powerful, God is all-good, and God exists) can't coexist with the reality of evil. Therefore, the thinking goes, an all-powerful and all-good God does not exist. For Christians, the challenge is to find a way to uphold all four claims. When we tackle this issue and try to argue that evil *can* exist alongside God, we create what's known as a **theodicy**—a philosophical attempt to explain how a good and all-powerful God can allow suffering and evil.

This is usually done by clarifying the nature of God's divine attributes. One of the oldest and most compelling arguments is the **free will theodicy** advocated early on by Augustine.[4] This theodicy argues that since humans have free will, the fault of evil rests on people and not on God. This theodicy modifies the statement that God is all-powerful, suggesting that God's power is self-restrained to give humans free will. God is still fundamentally all-powerful because God could simply not have given humans free will. But since God chose to create us that way, the consequences of our decisions must be respected in order for our wills to actually be free.

If you had to pick between vanilla and chocolate ice cream and you went for vanilla but the ice cream vendor gave you chocolate anyway, did you actually make a free choice? No, you just had the illusion of free will since you were asked something that seemed like a real choice. Free will counts *if and only if* we receive the consequences of our choices. Our God-given free will means we can choose or reject God and the things God wants for us. It begins with the fact that we are given agency to reject God, because God first wants to "set over against himself a free image of himself, and all without any compulsion on his part."[5] In other words, our freedom resides

4. Augustine, "On Free Choice of the Will (*De libero arbitrio*)," in *Augustine: Earlier Writings*, ed. J. H. S. Burleigh (Westminster John Knox Press), 102–217.

5. Hans Urs von Balthasar, *Spirit and Institution: Explorations in Theology IV*, trans. Edward T. Oakes (Ignatius Press, 1995), 339.

in God's openness to rejection. Theologian Hans Urs von Balthasar puts it well:

> God is always the one who has lovingly surrendered himself in freedom, who accordingly seeks a free and loving vessel [*Raumgeben*] for his love, which wants to pour itself into the heart. He does this so that he might have created freedom by his side, that he might "make his home" (Jn 14:23) with this created freedom even alongside his own infinite freedom. For he wants to be able to "beget" and "give birth to" this freedom (Jn 1:13; 3:5; 1 Jn 3:9) from the womb of his infinite and loving surrender (of the Father to the Son in the Holy Spirit).[6]

To share freedom with humanity, God intentionally became vulnerable to rejection. In fact, we can view the Spirit as an "infinite vulnerability" because the Spirit can be blocked, quenched, and grieved.[7] As Balthasar writes, "The Holy Spirit who has been sent to, and poured into, those who make room for him is the one who, as it were, is the naked core of eternal love, the most vulnerable point on which the human spirit directly touches the divine."[8] While we have the freedom to choose or reject God, this choice, and any other decision we make thereafter, is first rooted in God's own free choice.

Since free will requires us to face the outcomes of our choices, a free will theist could say that the current state of the world is due to the fall. The world is shaped by sin—it's a broken reality and not the way God intended it to be. Evil happens as a result of sin, and God doesn't step in to change outcomes, or else it would negate humanity's free will. For example, let's say someone plans to channel their inner Will Smith by rushing the stage of an awards ceremony to slap the host across the face. But to their dismay, as they approach the host, God stops them in their tracks. They completely freeze and can't move. Does the would-be slapper really have free will in this

6. Balthasar, *Spirit and Institution*, 340.
7. Balthasar, *Spirit and Institution*, 340.
8. Balthasar, *Spirit and Institution*, 340–41.

scenario? No. If the consequences of their actions are controlled, they aren't really free.

But what about personal and biblical occurrences of divine intervention? How could these ever come about if people *must* receive the consequences of their choices? In his book *Why We Pray*, theologian John Peckham answers this question by stating that we should consider the bigger picture of cosmic conflict between good and evil as described in the Bible. In this scenario, God has made a commitment that, in certain situations, asking for help through **petitionary prayer** (prayer that asks God for something) will open up moral pathways for God to create good or stop evil. When someone freely gives God the right to determine their outcomes—when they fully surrender to God's will—their petitionary prayers could give God the moral permission to take more direct action in response to those prayers. But even here, the divine action would not infringe on the free will of anyone else who is involved.

Peckham calls this tension between free outcomes and divine intervention the "influence aim problem." Like the problem of evil, the influence aim problem affirms four statements: (1) God is all-knowing, (2) God is all-good, (3) God is all-powerful, and (4) petitionary prayer might influence God to do some good that God might not have been able to do otherwise.[9] Peckham notes that there are many instances in Scripture when God *wants* to be gracious and forgiving (Ezra 18:23; Isa. 30:18; Joel 2:13; 2 Pet. 3:9) but waits on sinners to repent in order to provide moral or legal license to do so while upholding justice.[10] In all of those cases, God is still playing by the rules of free will that were determined upon creation.

Here, someone might ask, Why did God create evil in the first place? Why not create a world where evil can't exist? Let's think about this theologically. Augustine famously argued that evil exists as the privation (holding back) of good.[11] Some things exist not because

9. John Peckham, *Why We Pray: Understanding Prayer in the Context of Cosmic Conflict* (Baker Academic, 2024), 10.

10. Peckham, *Why We Pray*, 28.

11. Augustine, *Confessions* (Penguin Books, 1961), 147.

they were created but because something was withheld: Absolute zero is the absence of heat, and darkness is the absence of light. In Augustine's view, evil is thus the absence of good, and hell is the absence of God. So God did not create evil—it's not a thing that can be created. However, God *did* create the possibility for evil when God gave humans free will. The Tree of the Knowledge of Good and Evil symbolizes our God-given freedom to choose (Gen. 2).

If we are given the choice either to be in perfect community with God or to reject God, then the consequences of those choices will come about either by an affirmation (be in communion with God) or by a negation (reject God). If God is life and the giver of life, what happens when we reject God? We turn away from life and turn toward death; hence the wages of sin is death (Rom. 6:23). In fact, hell could be viewed not as a punishment from God but as the natural reality that comes from rejecting God, who is life. If you remove eternal life, you're left with eternal death. If you remove eternal love, you're left with eternal suffering. It's not that God makes us suffer—make no mistake, Scripture says God desires for all to be saved and even pleads for us to turn toward God (Exod. 18:32; 1 Tim. 2:3–4; 2 Pet. 3:9). It's that God honors the consequences of our decisions. If we decide to reject God, we receive hell. Evil is in every form some rejection of God. Evil is the negation of God, uncreated, and utterly opposed to the nature and work of God. God doesn't *let* bad things happen to us any more than a teacher lets students cheat on a test.

But while the free will objection absolves God of moral evil, what about natural evil, like a hurricane or tsunami that kills thousands of innocent people? How is natural evil a consequence of human sin? First, we should question if we can even call natural phenomena evil. Surely acts of nature do not have moral intent. But someone might object and say, "Nature isn't evil, but God is evil for causing the phenomena to occur as some sort of punishment." Someone else might argue that if God does not choose to intervene in cases of destructive natural phenomena, God is either not all-good, not all-powerful, or does not exist.

The theological response to these challenges would, once again, be free will. When Adam and Eve sinned, it wasn't just them who were cursed but creation too. The serpent was cursed to crawl on its belly (Gen. 3:14), the woman was cursed to feel pain in childbirth (v. 16), the ground was cursed and man was cursed to till it (vv. 17–18), and death entered the human experience (v. 19). The fallout from sin disrupted every important relationship: between people and God, between people and each other, and between people and the world around them. Natural evil isn't the result of a particular person's sin, nor is it used by God for retribution. It occurs because the world is fallen due to sin.

At this point we might look at the Old Testament God who caused the flood and burned down Sodom and Gomorrah. Those are significant issues that deal with another slew of questions (e.g., justice, judgment, the nature of reading ancient texts). I don't have the space to get into that here, but I'll leave a footnote that lists several good books on the topic for you to check out.[12] One thing we can know for sure, though, is what God's character is like because it was perfectly demonstrated by Christ. Because Jesus is the incarnate God, we know God is loving, gracious, kind, and sacrificial. We can see all of these characteristics demonstrated in the life, ministry, death, and resurrection of Jesus. Since God would rather die in our place than live without us, we know there must be more to the story. We know that God is the one who weeps with us in our suffering, just as Jesus wept with Mary and Martha (John 11:35). Vindictiveness is not in God's character. What's proven by Jesus in Scripture is

12. See Matthew Lynch and Helen Paynter, *Flood and Fury: Old Testament Violence and the Shalom of God* (IVP Academic, 2023); Paul Copan, *Is God a Moral Monster? Making Sense of the Old Testament God* (Baker Books, 2011); J. Richard Middleton, *Abraham's Silence: The Binding of Isaac, the Suffering of Job, and How to Talk Back to God* (Baker Academic, 2021); Greg Boyd, *Cross Vision: How the Crucifixion of Jesus Makes Sense of Old Testament Violence* (Fortress, 2017); Bradley Jersak, *A More Christlike God: A More Beautiful Gospel* (Plain Truth Ministries, 2015); L. Daniel Hawk, *The Violence of the Biblical God: Canonical Narrative and Christian Faith* (Eerdmans, 2019); and Tremper Longman III and John Walton, *The Lost World of the Flood: Mythology, Theology, and the Deluge Debate* (IVP Academic, 2018).

that we serve a just and compassionate God, not one who delights in our suffering.

Talking to a Silent God

While free will theodicy powerfully absolves God of moral culpability in regard to our suffering, are we sure it absolves God of moral indifference? It's easy to say that the best thing we can do when we suffer is to talk to God like Job does. But what if God is silent? In Scripture, it seems like Job has a direct line to God—but what if God's not responding to us?

In such cases, we should look at a few things regarding our own prayers. First, is what we're praying for aligned with God's will? Peckham writes, "Whether a request might be granted is contingent on whether it accords with God's *name* (i.e., God's character of perfect goodness and love) and thus whether it aligns with God's good will for all concerned, which takes into account all factors—including many unseen factors in the cosmic conflict."[13] We have to be honest with ourselves and ask if what we're asking God for is actually selfish and might work against God's will. That doesn't mean we shouldn't talk to God about everything; in fact, the opposite is true. Our prayers should embrace raw openness that lets God know what's on our mind. And we can do this through several types of prayer. We've already mentioned petitionary prayer, but there are also **prayers of lament**, which express grief, frustration, sorrow, or confusion to God (Job does this a lot); **prayers of confession**, in which a believer talks to God honestly about their sins, weaknesses, and struggles; and **prayers of examen**, in which a believer reflects on their daily thoughts, feelings, joys, and failures. We pray all these relationally to constantly stay in communion with God.

But as we petition God, we should make sure we're asking for the things God wants for us. We don't want God to bend to our wills; we want our wills to conform to God's. We're Christ's disciples, after all. Still, at times, our petitionary prayers can be sincere but

13. Peckham, *Why We Pray*, 108.

off-target. The things we're asking for might seem good and right to us, but they may not be part of God's bigger plan. This is why James says, "You ask and do not receive because you ask wrongly, in order to spend what you get on your pleasures" (James 4:3). When God is silent, perhaps God is subtly indicating, "This isn't what I have in mind for you."

Second, God's silence could show that it's not the right time for what we're asking for. Peckham again gives insight:

> Perhaps the timing is not right for God to grant a request initially, but conditions would be right later on (relative to the rules of engagement or otherwise), *if* one does not *lose hope and give up* in the meantime. In a case of seemingly unanswered prayer, God's answer might not be "no" but "not yet." Given this context, persevering prayer involves patience to wait on God's timing.[14]

We might not be ready for what we're asking for, but God knows when the right time will come. As the writer of Ecclesiastes tells us, "For everything there is a season and a time for every matter under heaven" (3:1).

Not too long ago, Mila (who's now eleven years old) asked Connie and me if she could have her own phone. I'm very open and honest with my daughter, so I expressed to her the dangers of having a phone at such a young age. I shared with her some studies that I had read that talked about how too much screen time can mess up a child's development. I told her, "You'll have a phone for the rest of your life, so if waiting to get a phone during these crucially formative years helps you be healthier in the long run, then that's probably the best thing to do." She understood. She still wants a phone, of course, but she knows it's better for her to hold off for now. She wasn't told "no" but rather "not yet." Sometimes God does the same with us.

Even as we acknowledge the possible inadequacies of our own prayers, we've all likely experienced such great anxiety during times

14. Peckham, *Why We Pray*, 119.

of crisis that it was hard to hear God through the intense volume of our burdens. In these situations, our minds get clouded and our spirits feel restless or defeated. What can we do then? First, we should acknowledge God's silence and admit that we're having trouble hearing God. Even David prayed,

> How long, O Lord? Will you forget me forever?
> How long will you hide your face from me? (Ps. 13:1)

I've prayed this prayer many times. It reminds me that we don't always need to live in triumph—sometimes the best thing to do is lament.

Once we've acknowledged God's silence, the next best thing to do might be to sit in stillness. We often talk so much in prayer that we don't even try to listen. Give silence a shot. Just as God told the psalmist, "Be still, and know that I am God" (Ps. 46:10), let's be still and sit with God. If you can't feel God's presence, sit anyway. God is there.

If we adopt a more contemplative posture, we might even end up finding God in unexpected places. As we go through our days, we might hear God through music or through the words of a friend. We might even see God in a sunrise or through the chattering of birds. God might be wanting us to stop, slow down, and pay attention to the Spirit in the mundane.

One practical, crucial thing we should do when we can't hear God is go back to Scripture and rehearse what we know to be true about God. We know that God is with us (Isa. 41:10), that God hears us (1 John 5:14), and that God is faithful (2 Tim. 2:13). While God didn't cause whatever crisis we're dealing with to occur, God can use the crisis to deepen our faith. Through it, we can learn to trust not just God's provision but who God is. God has proven to be good in the past, and we can believe God is still good in the present when things are looking dire. In fact, this seems to be Paul's main point when he says, "I have learned to be content with whatever I have. I know what it is to have little, and I know what it is to have plenty. In any and all circumstances I have learned the secret of being well-fed and of going hungry, of having plenty and of being in need. I can do all things through him who strengthens me" (Phil. 4:11–13). We often see verse 13 taken out of context as a verse that has to do with willpower. Instead, it's what Paul says when he thanks the church in Philippi for the gift he is given. He basically says, "This is nice, and thank you, but I don't actually need it. I've learned to trust God through the good times and the bad, when I have a lot or a little." It's an odd way to show gratitude, but we get Paul's point.

Finally, following the Spirit when it's dark sometimes requires a sacrifice of obedience. Paul tells us that we must walk by faith and not by sight (2 Cor. 5:7). Even if we feel nothing, sometimes the best thing to do is to just keep walking. Silence doesn't mean God has reneged on a promise. God's word remains true and trustworthy. I've always loved V. Raymond Edman's quote, "Never doubt in the dark what God told you in the light."[15] We must hold fast to the truths that were revealed to us in brighter times. We must take on a posture of holy stubbornness—a headstrongness that won't let the circumstances of today determine what we've known about God or confuse us about God's will for our lives.

One way we can rephrase Edman's quote to focus on following the Spirit when it's dark is "If you can't see the light, remember what the light looked like, and follow that." If we follow the light that we remember, we'll know the Spirit is guiding our steps even when we can't see what's ahead.

Finding Meaning in the Silence

I've always found the beginning of Ecclesiastes to be striking, and it's pertinent to our conversation about crisis and anxiety. Verse 2 says,

> Vanity of vanities, says the Teacher,
> vanity of vanities! All is vanity.

15. V. Raymond Edman, *The Disciplines of Life* (Victor Books, 1975), 33.

For an even gloomier take, check out the NIV translation:

> "Meaningless! Meaningless!"
> says the Teacher.
> "Utterly meaningless!
> Everything is meaningless."

Depending on which Bible translation you're reading, you'll see "vanity," "meaningless," and sometimes "futility" stand in for the Hebrew word *hevel* (הֶבֶל). Because *hevel* is a picturesque word that means "vapor," "mist," or "breath," we can get a broader sense of what the writer of Ecclesiastes is getting at by taking all these translations together. Everything, the Teacher says, is futile, meaningless, and vain. Everything is like a vapor, here for a moment and gone in the next. The things we strive for—money, success, pleasure—are empty. These things are *hevel*—beautiful but fleeting and ultimately unsatisfying.

Sometimes Ecclesiastes feels to me like the Bible's misfit, like that goth cousin who shows up at family reunions talking about death and listening to The Cure. The Teacher of Ecclesiastes is dark! He seems more like Albert Camus than a prophet of God. Unlike much of the rest of the Bible, Ecclesiastes takes us on a journey through the difficulties of life: hard work that leads only to death, wisdom that doesn't ensure success, fleeting pleasures, and injustices that remain unaddressed. The book revels in the dissonance of unanswered questions.[16] It's almost as if Ecclesiastes pulls us aside and asks, "Be honest—none of this makes sense, does it?" But this unrestrained exploration of the hard questions of life is precisely why it belongs in the Bible. I'd even argue that this exploration is one of Scripture's best responses to our crippling anxieties.

16. William Brown, *Wisdom's Wonder: Character, Creation, and Crisis in the Bible's Wisdom Literature* (Eerdmans, 2014), 3.

The Wisdom of Dissonance

Trusting God despite not having the answers seems to be a recurring theme of the wisdom books of the Bible. As a biblical genre, the **Wisdom tradition** offers practical and philosophical guidance for living well in God's world by exploring questions about life, morality, and suffering. The main wisdom books are Job, Ecclesiastes, and Proverbs. While Psalms and Song of Songs are often considered part of this tradition too, these two books also cross into other genres like poetry. The Wisdom tradition is universal; people can apply its teachings across different cultures and eras without needing to know the ins and outs of Jewish history and culture. In fact, Old Testament scholar David Penchansky said the authors "did not intend their writing for Israel only. It was meant for all people and for all time. It was not meant for Israel in particular, so the first three books scarcely give a hint of the authors' own national identity."[17] These books invite readers from any time or place to engage in deeper spiritual and existential thought. Even though the wisdom books aren't uniquely Jewish, they consistently emphasize dependence on God.

Key to understanding the Wisdom tradition is our need to recognize the openness and uncertainty of the wisdom writers when it comes to theological problems.[18] Just like we noticed in Job and Ecclesiastes, these writers don't kick off their books with simple answers to complex issues; instead, they dive headfirst into the harsh realities of their problems, even questioning established beliefs. They're the opposite of self-help books. We'll never find a book called *The Ten Habits of Highly Suffering People* by Job. Rather, we see Job wondering why he's experiencing so much suffering when conventional wisdom says God runs the universe justly. The wisdom writers embrace these sorts of tensions and conflicting messages not because they enjoy being in the dark but because they understand that some aspects of life emerge only after the sun sets.

17. David Penchansky, *Understanding Wisdom Literature: Conflict and Dissonance in the Hebrew Text* (Eerdmans, 2012), 12.
18. Penchansky, *Understanding Wisdom Literature*, 96.

Sometimes, unresolved tensions can even lead us to see multiple conflicting voices *within* a single book. For instance, Ecclesiastes features three unique voices. The term "Teacher" in Ecclesiastes is derived from the Hebrew *Qoheleth* (קֹהֶלֶת), which translates to "teacher" or "preacher." Penchansky sees Ecclesiastes presenting three distinct Qoheleths in conversation. The first voice is the "Pessimistic Qoheleth."[19] This is the voice that opens the book with "all is vanity" (1:2)—a capricious voice that questions life's meaning. The second voice is the "Fear God Qoheleth."[20] Wrapped in practical advice, this Qoheleth emphasizes the importance of fearing God and looks for God's influence in everyday scenarios. Last, we have the third voice, the "Enjoy Life Qoheleth,"[21] who encourages readers to seek joy in life's simple pleasures, such as in the well-known verse that says to "eat, drink, and be merry" (8:15 KJV). This Qoheleth wants us to remember that God has blessed us with a good life, so we should make the most of it. These three voices jockey back and forth, vying for interpretative control of the text.

Some scholars think these differing perspectives are deliberately inconsistent. I like this view. Given that Wisdom literature aims to showcase internal dialogues and the struggles associated with particular issues, it's possible that these voices intentionally belong to the same narrator.[22] Maybe the idea is for us to hold these conflicting perspectives together and to embrace the dissonances they create, which might even be cathartic for those who are suffering and tired of easy answers. Qoheleth's struggle validates us in our own. We're not crazy; life *is* hard!

When we take the three perspectives together, we see Ecclesiastes giving voice to the unspoken doubts and questions that many of us hold but hesitate to express. The unresolved dialogue disrupts our penchant for quick answers and challenges the idea that we can control our circumstances or discover life's meaning on our own terms.

19. Penchansky, *Understanding Wisdom Literature*, 51.
20. Penchansky, *Understanding Wisdom Literature*, 51.
21. Penchansky, *Understanding Wisdom Literature*, 51.
22. Craig Bartholomew, *Ecclesiastes* (Baker Academic, 2014), 79.

After searching for any inherent meaning in life, Qoheleth clears the way for us to recognize what truly matters: "Fear God, and keep his commandments, for that is the whole duty of everyone" (Eccles. 12:13). Qoheleth sees the futility of our self-interest and encourages us to let go of our grand ambitions and relentless striving. True meaning doesn't stem from what we build, own, or learn but from our relationship with our Creator. The fear of God is not about being afraid of what God might do to us—it's embracing a posture of reverent awe, respect, and wholehearted trust in God. Fearing God is recognizing that God is God and we are not. Ecclesiastes dispels our illusions and directs us to God, the only source of genuine meaning.

That's good stuff. Okay, Ecclesiastes, cue up "Friday I'm in Love" next on the playlist, and pull up a chair at the dinner table. You belong here.

A Meaningless Life or Purposeless Play?

Let's take a page from Qoheleth's book and have an unrestrained chat about meaning and anxiety. When we're stuck without answers to our questions, it's natural to feel some anxiety-fueled **dread** creep in—an overwhelming feeling of fear or worry about what might come to pass. Unlike sudden fear, dread builds up gradually through anticipation. It's that heavy, sinking sensation that something bad is looming ahead. We feel unsettled and vulnerable, like things are out of our control. While the wisdom writers have shown us the importance of trusting God and accepting the unknown, how can we reframe our thinking to help alleviate an existential sense of dread?

Some theologians have proposed that the best way to address existential dread is through play, what James Evans Jr. describes as "a set of activities or practices that occurs in the interstices between freedom and structure, between the subject(ive) and object(ive), between creation and imitation."[23] Through play, we get to explore, express ourselves, and connect with others not for any material reward but simply for the fun of it. We can think of **play** as participating in

23. James H. Evans Jr., *Playing* (Fortress, 2010), 11.

voluntary activities shaped by imagination, creativity, and mutually agreed-upon rules. When we play, we engage in a purposelessness that feels purposeful. The stakes seem significant in the act of playing, but in reality, they are either trivial or not there at all. You should see me when I play *Mario Kart*—nothing in the world is more important than beating my friends, family, and especially students. If I have to dodge a blue shell by using a mushroom at the last possible second, then so be it.

Play also helps us grow and adjust socially as human beings. Social psychologist Jonathan Haidt recently put forward a compelling argument that part of the reason Gen Z has grown in anxiety and depression is because they are the first generation to fully experience the "great rewiring" of childhood.[24] Around 2010, he argues, childhood shifted from play-based to phone-based as smartphones were adopted into every part of life.[25] Through play, children—and mammals in general—acquire essential skills they'll need to be successful as adults. The repeated activity, constant feedback, and ability to fail in low-stakes environments allow children to test things out and gain skills as they look after themselves and each other.[26] A play-based childhood involves kids spending their time synchronously playing with other kids in real life.[27] In contrast, a phone-based childhood sees children fixated on screens, interacting with others asynchronously and making a profile of themselves for others to see. The chronic social comparisons that happen on social media and the lack of real human contact create in children a tremendous amount of anxiety to live up to unrealistic social standards and trends.[28] Posting on social media is not low stakes for kids and teens, because the posts can have real social repercussions within friend groups. Because the kids and teens can't fail in a safe place, their emotional and psychological

24. Jonathan Haidt, *The Anxious Generation: How the Great Rewiring of Childhood Is Causing an Epidemic of Mental Illness* (Penguin Books, 2024), 7.
25. Haidt, *Anxious Generation*, 7.
26. Haidt, *Anxious Generation*, 52.
27. Haidt, *Anxious Generation*, 53.
28. Haidt, *Anxious Generation*, 54.

growth is extremely inhibited. Play is necessary for our healthy human development, and when it is missing, there can be serious developmental consequences.

When we look at play from a theological perspective, it becomes clear that "playing" with God can be an amazing relational aim. Play occurs when we're living peacefully in a state of shalom. And when we're dealing with our hurts, anxieties, and insecurities, play helps to create shalom in us. Imagine a family playing together in the middle of a war-torn area. For them, play is more than just an escape; it's a refuge. Even when everything around them is marked by destruction, the family can enjoy each other in play. In play, they're safe and free.

Similarly, when we engage in play with God, our relationship is free of agendas. We're not seeking anything from God; we're simply relishing our time spent with God. It's the Creator taking pleasure in creation, and creation delighting in its Creator. **Play theology** thus views play as a lens to understand God, creation, purpose, and worship. At the heart of this theology is the idea that play is an essential way to get into deeper communion with God. We exist to love God and to be loved by God—to enjoy God relationally. This, I would argue, is the purest way to understand our own purpose.

Theologian Jürgen Moltmann reminds us that humans naturally seek to understand the purpose of events and the meaning of life. However, as we've mentioned earlier, events often seem random, making it tough to find clear reasons for why certain things happen. In our quest for meaning, we might end up in "a desert of absurdity."[29] Our search might lead us to discover only vanity, which might push us toward **existential absurdism**—the belief that the universe is silent and indifferent, bearing no inherent meaning or purpose, so that our existence is meaningless. Or, Moltmann argues, our search could lead us to believe that the world has an innate "purposeless purpose" that's connected to its Creator through sheer relationality, or play.

29. Jürgen Moltmann, *Theology of Play*, trans. Reinhard Ulrich (Harper & Row, 1972), 16.

While this second option is more creatively generative and fits well into our theology, there's still no discernible reason for anything to exist at all.[30] At this point, we might wonder, "Why does creation exist if it serves no purpose?" Moltmann answers, "When he (God) creates something that is not god but also not nothing, then this must have its ground not in itself but in God's good will or pleasure. Hence the creation is God's play, a play of his groundless and inscrutable wisdom. It is the realm in which God displays his glory."[31] Creation is not essential but is still cherished by God. It's not necessary for God's essence, nor was it made from God's essence. Creation didn't have to exist, yet it does. For Moltmann, creation is, like play itself, "meaningful but not necessary."[32] We must understand the innate purpose of the universe and God's relationship to it, or we'll be caught in a "crisis of living" where nothing makes sense and everything is useless.[33]

Play theology also helps us view ourselves as meaningful in ourselves. We do not earn the right to be loved by God; God loves us just because. We are defined not by our actions or our achievements but by being God's children. As Moltmann writes, "We too are evidently supposed to be busy with something, as if our existence were justified or rendered beautiful by this. The opposite is true: Our existence is justified and made beautiful before we are able to do or fail to do anything."[34] Before anything else, play theology focuses on the nature and significance of those participating in play. Both God and humans hold intrinsic meaning. We are valuable and made beautiful by God because God finds joy in us. Therefore, we can say that humanity and all of creation possesses inherent worth, and that the Creator engages playfully with creation.

Through this framing, we can find hope in suffering and peace in mystery. We can see that bad things happen because the world is

30. Moltmann, *Theology of Play*, 16.
31. Moltmann, *Theology of Play*, 17.
32. Moltmann, *Theology of Play*, 17.
33. Moltmann, *Theology of Play*, 19.
34. Moltmann, *Theology of Play*, 21.

free, but that doesn't mean we aren't valuable and loved by God. Love is a choice made freely, and with that freedom comes the potential for pain. In Christ, God experiences everything that humanity goes through and even more, becoming the ultimate victim of free will's consequences. Christ's suffering isn't without purpose. Moltmann says it serves two significant roles: It shows us that God stands in solidarity with us in our pain, and it offers us atonement, lifting the burden of guilt from our shoulders.[35] In our own times of suffering, we can find peace in knowing that God is neither far away nor indifferent. God is a Father and a brother who feels our pain and walks alongside us through every hardship. In the peace of this truth, we learn to trust God, even when it's dark.

Worship as Holy Play

For the rest of this chapter, I'd like to argue that the spiritual discipline of worship is not only formative, as discussed in the last chapter, but beneficial for our holistic well-being and essential for combating today's pressures and anxieties. If we look at the way we described play above, we can view worship as "holy play" with God and the church. At its core, worship consists of being drawn into the presence of the Holy Spirit. That means that, like play, worship is not utilitarian. Worship is not about profit or production (at least it shouldn't be) but about dwelling in the presence of God. In worship, we enter a sacred space where we enact God's story of reconciliation through structured, symbolic, and imaginative rituals. All of us—everyone in the worshiping community—are drawn together to sing, pray, confess, and celebrate God. When we're together, the eternal Spirit breaks into our present so we can glimpse a foretaste of what is to come.[36] We don't simply rehearse the coming kingdom of shalom but actively participate in it. As the church proclaims the arrival of

35. Jürgen Moltmann, *Jesus Christ for Today's World* (Fortress, 1994), 38.

36. In theology, this is called prolepsis, the idea that God's future promises can be experienced in the present. For more on this, see Glenn Packiam, *Worship and the World to Come: Exploring Christian Hope in Contemporary Worship* (IVP Academic,

God's kingdom, genuine hope for the future begins to shape and influence our current situation.[37] In worship, what is to come affects our present day.

Worship creates a charged space where the Spirit of God moves freely about, and anything is possible when the Spirit is present. Pentecostals have long believed that healings and miracles happen when the Spirit is at work,[38] but Christians from all denominations can agree that if it is God's will and we're open and expectant, extraordinary things can happen. In worship we thus play with God and are made whole by virtue of being in God's presence. We are holistically healed—mind, body, and soul. While God can (and often does) heal us physically, for an anxious generation, much of what needs to be healed is mental and emotional. This is especially significant for our conversation about suffering.

In his book *Worship in an Age of Anxiety*, J. Michael Jordan says the church has the potential to be a sanctuary for healing in all aspects, including anxiety. Yet he points out that many churches tend to implement contemporary strategies in their production, programming, and ministerial efforts that inadvertently add to and sustain anxiety. He explains that evangelical pastors and evangelists engage in what he calls an "anxiety-repentance-relief" cycle, where people feel pressured to confess their anxieties, repent from the sins or actions causing them, and find relief from those anxieties.[39] The problem with the anxiety-repentance-relief cycle is not that people are seeking relief from anxiety through spiritual alignment but that this cycle can be manipulative, exacerbating rather than healing anxiety.[40] It's as if pastors and evangelists use anxiety to get desired responses from their congregants. In some ways, the cycle promotes the exploitation of anxiety rather than genuinely dealing with it.

2020), 181. See also Steven Félix-Jäger, *Renewal Worship: A Theology of Pentecostal Doxology* (IVP Academic, 2022), 39–40.

37. Félix-Jäger, *Renewal Worship*, 39.

38. J. Rodman Williams, *Renewal Theology: Systematic Theology from a Charismatic Perspective* (Zondervan, 1996), 256.

39. Jordan, *Worship in an Age of Anxiety*, 35.

40. Jordan, *Worship in an Age of Anxiety*, 54–55.

This cycle is also present in evangelical worship when worship teams craft an atmosphere of spectacle.[41] The production, intended to immerse worshipers and help them concentrate on God, can sometimes lead to distractions instead, preventing worshipers from truly hearing God or being fully engaged in worship.[42] The danger of churches becoming totalizing spaces is that they can skew toward performance rather than participation. In such a church culture, worshipers can end up being more like consumers of a spiritual event rather than engaging in a community of faith. High-quality production can create powerful emotional peaks that seem like spiritual moments, leading folks to mistakenly link God's presence with how intense the experience is.[43] This makes faith reliant on stimulation, causing mundane worship practices (like silence, lament, prayer, and the sacraments) to feel lacking. And when anxious worshipers don't respond experientially in the expected way, they may feel an extra layer of pressure or judgment that stems from comparisons.

Many of us in Pentecostal or evangelical circles have heard testimonies from churches all over the world where the anxiety-repentance-relief strategy actually works. Certainly, there are instances where people have found relief from their anxiety because they repented from something that was causing their anxiety. We know anxiety does not always come about from sin, but what if there's a particular case where it does? If someone is reared in evangelicalism, speaks the language of anxiety-repentance-relief, and then finds relief, isn't that okay? Even if we make room for this exception, we can say that while the cycle is beneficial to some in evangelicalism, it shouldn't be applied universally as the primary way in which anxiety is dealt with in the church.

Even with these critiques, Jordan believes worship can become a space for healing. For example, sacraments and the liturgical calendar can help anxious people connect with the larger Christian story. When we share Communion on the Lord's day or celebrate the incarnation while anticipating Christ's return during Advent,

41. Jordan, *Worship in an Age of Anxiety*, 77.
42. Jordan, *Worship in an Age of Anxiety*, 78.
43. Jordan, *Worship in an Age of Anxiety*, 111.

we acknowledge that we belong to something greater than ourselves and we embrace something that is meaning-making in our own lives. These communal practices shift the focus away from us as individuals and direct our attention toward God's community, which can provide structure and stability for those dealing with anxiety.[44]

In worship, we should avoid forcing a general-purpose emotional script (starting high and celebratory, ending deep and contemplative). Instead, we could employ things like lament or prayers of confession in our worship, which give people the space to sit with God instead of providing a quick emotional fix.[45] One time during a chapel service at my university, we brought in one of my friends, a brilliant historian, to preach. She has a PhD in church history and has authored many books, but she really is a Pentecostal revivalist at heart, so she often stretches people to experience God in new ways. During this particular chapel service, after her introduction, she prayed. In the middle of the prayer she stopped and asked everyone in the room to sit silently and listen to God. This wasn't just a moment of silence; she stayed in the silence for longer than anyone expected. A couple of minutes passed, and the whole auditorium remained silent. At first, it was awkward. Students shuffled and looked around, uncertain. But she was patient. After another minute or so, we could hear students whimpering around the room. Some students began to cry. Others sat in stunned silence. A couple of folks laughed—a deep, free kind of laughter, the kind we call joy in the Spirit. No one looked at their phones.

I was so surprised by what took place. In such a fast-paced, media-saturated world, we stopped and sat in silent prayer together. Pentecostals are known for being loud and sometimes unruly. But this was a holy hush. We didn't just hear *about* God—we risked awkwardness and social embarrassment to encounter the Spirit through corporate stillness. My friend's prayer made room for the students' tears, joys, and unpolished prayers, and no one felt pressured to perform. In a

44. Jordan, *Worship in an Age of Anxiety*, 92.
45. Jordan, *Worship in an Age of Anxiety*, 92.

university setting, my friend disrupted academic stiffness with Spirit-led imagination.

Recently, my church held a special Good Friday worship service that also carved out space for healing. It was a night service, and the room was dimly lit. Our pastor had the idea to put a wooden cross, unadorned and raw, at the center of the room—not on a stage or elevated platform but right in the middle of us, within arm's reach. The seating was arranged in the round, all of us facing inward, surrounding the cross. I was playing in the band, and we set up behind the congregants, removed from the spotlight. It made worship feel less like a performance and more like a communal prayer centered around the cross. The theme of the night was how Jesus breaks every chain.

As people entered the space, they were handed a two-foot length of metal chain. We began worshiping, singing songs but leaving room between sets for prayer, Scripture reading, prophetic words, and testimonies from anyone who wanted to share. At one point, when the music died down a bit, we were invited to bring our chains and lay them at the foot of the cross. At first, everyone was still. Ambient sounds were playing, and people were swaying with eyes closed, praying individually. Then I heard the clinking of metal on wood. I heard another chain drop, and another. Soon, all the chains were at the foot of the cross. When I opened my eyes, I saw people kneeling in prayer, some weeping. Some sat in silence, and others laid hands on each other in prayer. After a little while, the room went still again, we prayed communally, and then we began to sing another song.

This was one of the most powerful worship services I ever attended. By the end of the night, I felt like a ton of weight had been lifted off my shoulders. So many people prayed and demonstrated love for one another as we honored Christ together. Many of the congregants talked to us afterward about feeling relief and healing. As we dwelled in God's presence, we were blessed. God was blessed. This sort of healing is always possible in worship; perhaps we just need a little more openness to recognize it.

Worship, sacraments, call-and-response, and communal prayers all have structure, but when we approach them with openness and joy, they can turn into holy play. The "rules" of worship (like the rules of a game) create an environment for freedom. In worship, the pressures of contingent outcomes fade away and we can be vulnerable. We can sing off-key, lift our hands, cry, kneel, or express words of praise or sorrow that we might not voice otherwise. When we do this together, we foster a sense of communal trust that says, *You see me. I feel safe here. I'm not alone.*

Engaging worship as play allows us to joyfully practice our faith in the company of God and each other. When we participate in creative, joyful worship, we come to know God not only as a judge or ruler but as a loving Father, brother, and trustworthy friend. In a world filled with anxiety, worship as play says God has already won the game. It's a small act of resistance against a world of despair. It's a proclamation that we'll follow the Spirit even when it's dark.

Conclusion

At the start of this chapter, I told you about my family's big move to California. But in a classic Wisdom literature move, I left you in the tension of an unfinished story. So let's pick it up here.

The school I worked at went under; we had nothing but debt; and the potential of moving back to Florida, defeated, became more likely every day. But a miracle was on the horizon. Through this whole ordeal, I was feverishly applying for other jobs. I was throwing out applications everywhere, even if I wasn't totally qualified. There was a nearby Pentecostal university that was looking for a professor and department chair. It seemed like a good fit—I was a Pentecostal theologian, after all, but at this point, I had only worked as an adjunct professor and high school teacher, so jumping all the way to department chair seemed like a long shot. But after several interviews, campus visits, and teaching samples, I got the job. And after months of anxious uncertainty, my new title would be Assistant Professor of Theology and Worship, and Chair of the Worship Arts and Media program. My new role would be to raise up worship pastors so that they could help others be drawn into God's presence. How fitting!

Looking back, I realize that my story was never outside of God's reach. The God I met in my prayers, Scripture reading, and worship was the same God who guided me in the dark. It was tough to recognize then, but I now know that what felt like silence was the grace of God at work. I didn't deserve to lose everything, but I also didn't deserve to gain a job that was a few steps above my experience. God was gracious and good, and in my despair, God found a way to bless me beyond anything I could hope for. But not every story wraps up with a happy ending like this one. In those cases, we must learn to accept what's beyond our control and trust God anyway. Along the way, we may yet find healing. After all, Job doesn't embark on a quest where the end result would be healing; rather, the journey itself brings him a sort of healing through acceptance.

This chapter has taken us through several movements: from suffering to silence, wisdom, play, and worship. As we lament and revel in the dissonance of what's going on in our lives, we can rest assured that Jesus will be on the other side of our crisis. Through viewing worship as a form of holy play—a sacred space where healing, imagination, and divine encounter are made possible—we learn to find meaning and acceptance even while we are still walking through darkness. Perhaps the greatest takeaway from this chapter is this: Following the Spirit when it's dark doesn't always mean knowing where we're going. Sometimes it means remembering what the light looked like and following that. The Spirit still moves in the dark. And God is still good—even there.

KEY WORDS

- **anxiety**: A future-oriented, unrestrained worry
- **dread**: An overwhelming feeling of fear or worry about what might come to pass

- **existential absurdism**: The belief that the universe is silent and indifferent, bearing no inherent meaning or purpose, so that our existence is meaningless
- **free will theodicy**: A theodicy that argues since humans have free will, the fault of evil rests on people and not on God
- **petitionary prayer**: Prayer that asks God for something
- **play**: Participating in voluntary activities shaped by imagination, creativity, and mutually agreed-upon rules
- **play theology**: The view of play as a lens to understand God, creation, purpose, and worship
- **prayer of confession**: A type of prayer where a believer talks to God honestly about their own sins, weaknesses, and struggles
- **prayer of examen**: A type of prayer where a believer reflects on their daily thoughts, feelings, joys, and failures
- **prayer of lament**: A type of prayer where a believer expresses grief, frustration, sorrow, or confusion to God
- **problem of evil**: One of the best-known philosophical challenges against the existence of a good and all-powerful God
- **theodicy**: A philosophical attempt to explain how a good and all-powerful God can allow suffering and evil
- **Wisdom tradition**: A biblical genre that offers practical and philosophical guidance for living well in God's world by exploring various questions about life, morality, and suffering

DISCUSSION QUESTIONS

- Have you ever experienced a season where you felt like you did everything right but things still fell apart? Did you sense God's presence or absence during that time?
- In what ways might practicing prayers of lament or examen deepen your relationship with God?

- How does the concept of holy play reframe your understanding of worship? When have you felt most "at play" in God's presence?

REFLECTION EXERCISE

Compose a prayer or poem of lament, naming your grief, confusion, or doubt in a season of silence. Share it with a trusted friend or spiritual mentor and invite them to pray with you.

Conclusion

Being Led Through an Age of Discernment

Have you ever experienced something, judged it negatively, and then rethought it from a different vantage point and ended up liking it? This happens to me all the time. When I was . . . a young boy, I used to think the band My Chemical Romance was lame. At that time, I was really into metal, and MCR was just too soft! Then when I became a man, I put away my childish biases and listened again to *The Black Parade* album. The punky drums, theatrical arrangements, and passionate vocals of Gerard Way got me. My nostalgia went into high gear, and it was then that I realized MCR wasn't lame, but actually one of the greatest bands of all time. I had to reframe my thinking from "If it's not metal, it's lame" to "I bet this album is gonna bring me back." Once I did that, I became open-minded and listened to MCR afresh. I realized how good they were and that I actually liked them.

In the same way, we can reframe how we're thinking about our current era. Instead of thinking about the world as a chaotic age of pluralism, what if we thought about it as an age of discernment? In both framings, we're observing the same facts—the world is full of competing narratives, mis- and disinformation, political tribalism, and fear of the unknown. The difference is that we stop thinking about these realities as events that are happening to us and instead as the context in which God has called us to live, flourish, and minister. We shift from being passively overwhelmed to actively engaged.

Reframing this age moves us from merely naming and surviving a condition (many voices, many truths, many paths) to embracing a spiritual commission. While pluralism says we're surrounded by scary and unsettling differences, discernment says we're invited to explore these differences and respond with wisdom. In the Spirit, we can approach things with curiosity instead of defensiveness and with wisdom rather than withdrawal. As we practice the spiritual discipline of discernment through prayer, Scripture reading, and worship, we'll be formed spiritually, and as we allow the Spirit to work in our lives, we'll be empowered by the gift of discernment. Then, as Spirit-empowered discerners, we will no longer be mere witnesses to cultural fragmentation but faithful witnesses of Christ amid the chaos of our present age.

Most importantly, reframing this age takes the focus off of us (or the world) and puts it squarely on the Holy Spirit. Our perspective switches from a fear-inducing worldly frame to a hope-building pneumatological one. This world is God's, and the Spirit is present and active in it now. The Spirit is at work today in the discerning hearts of every believer who is engaging with the world as it truly is while looking ahead to what it can be.

Throughout this book we set up a progression from diagnosis to discipleship, and from the world's noise to Spirit-led responses. Part 1, "Hearing God," explored the cultural, theological, and philosophical landscape of our present pluralistic age, arguing that it is defined by secularism, competing narratives, and mis- and disinformation. In these times, prayer and Scripture reading can provide us with spiritual grounding. Then, in part 2, "Following the Spirit," we shifted our focus toward action. Even through political tribalism and personal crises, the spiritual discipline of worship can help us see and follow the Spirit. Together, this progression illustrates that discernment is not merely about surviving; it's our calling for such a time as this.

ONE FINAL REFLECTION EXERCISE

At the start of this book, I argued that discernment is the crucial spiritual gift and discipline of our time. As the book comes to a close, I'd like to invite you to do a bit of spiritual inventory. On a scale from 1 to 10, how would you rate your ability to:

- Hear God's voice amid competing messages?
- Make decisions rooted in prayer rather than pressure?
- Sense and respond to the Spirit's promptings?
- Distinguish truth from distortion in your faith tradition?

Whether you find yourself at a 2 or an 8, that's okay! This is about formation, not perfection. What practice, rhythm, or habit could help you grow by just one step in the next thirty days?

As you go forward, remember: Discernment is something you practice, not something you master. And when we practice discernment, we become more attuned to the Spirit, who is already speaking, already guiding, and already near. Let's tap into what the Spirit is doing. Let's walk on and listen well.

Index

Acts 2, 14–16, 62, 73
allegiance, 132, 135, 138–39, 142
  pledge of, 120–21
  political, 133–34, 148
  ultimate, 46
anxiety, 22, 152–53, 161, 163, 167–68, 172–74, 176–77
authority, 13, 21, 48, 85, 87, 93, 95, 104, 109, 122–23, 125, 136, 148

buffered self, 36–37, 51

church, 13–18, 35, 48, 58, 64, 80, 82, 105–6, 124, 126, 128, 144, 146–47, 151, 171–74
  invisible, 14, 23
  visible, 14–15, 23
confirmation bias, 90, 100, 103
critical thinking, 108–9
culture, 6–8, 13n17, 29, 40, 45, 51, 56, 71–73, 98, 105, 113, 119, 121, 123, 135, 141, 165, 174
  decultured, 103–4
  interpreting, 4–5, 22
  theology of, 3

discernment, ix, 3, 9–10, 17, 20, 22–23, 29–30, 32, 46, 48–51, 55, 73, 79–80, 109, 112–13, 142
  age of, 181–83
  spiritual discipline of, 18–19
  spiritual gift of, 18–19
disenchantment, 35, 51
disinformation, 5, 21, 86, 99–101, 107, 113–14, 182
dominion theology, 3, 122–25, 144, 148
dread, 22, 167, 177

ecclesiology, 14, 23
exclusivism, 70, 82
existential absurdism, 169, 178
experts, 85–86, 89, 91–95, 109

free will, 12, 69n20, 154–60, 171, 178
  theodicy, 160, 178
fundamentalism, 8, 104

gematria, 132–33, 149
globalization, 7–8, 23, 40, 41n31, 51
glocality, 29, 40, 51, 55
glossolalia, 28–29, 51

grace, 65, 107, 125–26, 177
cheap, 105, 113
costly, 105, 113
prevenient, 82n49

Holy Spirit, 3, 10, 12, 15–16, 23, 27–28, 62, 69, 72, 81, 109, 125, 136, 156, 171, 182
paraclete, 17
universal, 66, 73, 76

identity, 21, 29, 36, 38, 51, 64, 121–22, 127–30, 133–37, 139–49
national, 119–20, 165
politics, 140–41, 149
immanent frame, 38–39, 42, 51–52
incarnation, 10–11, 57, 62, 67, 82, 131, 173
inclusivism, 71–72, 82
interdenominational, 13, 15, 17

kingdom of God, 72, 120, 123, 134–35, 139n25, 149
kitsch, 104, 112–13

labels, 121, 129–31, 133, 141
lectio divina, 78–79, 82–83, 126
liturgy, 43, 52

"many tongues" thesis, 72–73
media, 7, 87, 94–95, 99–100, 174, 176
digital, 5
social, 20, 41, 43, 46, 86, 89–92, 95, 101–2, 106, 108, 168
misinformation, 5, 9, 20–21, 86, 99–101, 103–4, 113–14, 182
modern political lying, 95, 97–98, 114

naming, 122, 126–29, 133–34, 145, 179, 182
family name, 131, 149
narratives, 7, 20, 54, 69, 82, 100, 182
nationalism, 8, 9, 147
news pundits, 89, 114

Pentecostal, 10, 12–15, 17, 27–28, 48, 70, 93, 130, 143, 173–74, 176
perspicuity of Scripture, 80–81, 83
play, 167–72, 177–78
holy, 22, 171, 176–77, 179
theology, 170, 178
pluralism, 3, 19, 33, 54, 57, 66, 86, 182
age of, 2, 4–5, 9, 22–23, 30, 181
global, 54, 58, 81
religious, 6, 20, 56, 60–61, 67, 70, 83, 130
pneumatology, 10, 23
political, 5, 8, 21, 29, 32, 42, 74, 86–89, 91, 94–98, 100–02, 122, 136, 144, 150
allegiance, 120, 133–34, 148
buzzwords, 137–40
idols, 147
tribalism, 21, 121, 141, 142–43, 182
post-truth, 20, 86–87, 92, 95–96, 99, 105–6, 109–10, 112–14
pragmatism, 96–97, 114
vulgar, 97, 114
prayer, 13, 18, 20–23, 29, 46–47, 49–51, 55, 62–63, 76, 78–80, 86, 107, 111–12, 115, 127, 150, 154, 160–62, 175, 177, 179, 182–83
of confession, 160, 178
of examen, 160, 178
of lament, 160, 173–74, 178
petitionary, 157, 178
problem of evil, 154–55, 157, 178

reductionism, 9, 133, 141
relativism, 9
repentance, 143, 149, 172, 173

salvation, 55, 57–58, 60–61, 65–66, 68–71, 80, 82–83, 123, 131

secular, 5, 9, 20, 29, 32, 38–39, 41, 46, 51–52, 182
  liturgy, 43, 45, 52, 114
  Secularity 1, 33–34, 41–42, 52
  Secularity 2, 34, 35, 42, 52
  Secularity 3, 29, 36–39, 41–42, 51, 52, 86
  spirituality, 44–45, 52
shalom, 123–24, 149, 169, 171
social contract, 135, 149
social imaginary, 34, 36, 52
social media algorithms, 90, 101
spiritual reading, 20, 51, 55, 76–79, 81–83, 110

Taylor, Charles, 29, 32–40, 42
theodicy, 155, 160, 178
  free will, 160, 178
theophany, 61–62, 83
Trinity, 10, 17, 57, 62, 83
triumphalism, 13
truth, 5, 17, 20–21, 32, 47, 52, 54–55, 57, 68–71, 76, 78, 81–82, 86–87, 89, 91–92, 95–110, 112–14, 120, 126, 145, 163, 171, 182–83
  authentic, 105, 113
  correspondence theory of, 96, 105, 113
  kitschification of, 86, 103–04, 112

Wisdom tradition, 165, 178
wokeness, 140, 149
Word of Faith theology, 126–27
worship, 11–13, 21–22, 27, 44, 62, 64, 66, 108, 121–22, 132–33, 142–49, 153, 171–79, 182

Yong, Amos, 70–76